M000014638

Extreme Love

Extreme Love

Discover and Experience God's Love for You

BARBOUR
PUBLISHING

Our mission is to publish and distribute inspirational products offering exceptional value and biblical encouragement to the masses.

Member of the
Evangelical Christian
Publishers Association

Be absolutely certain that <u>our Lord loves you</u> devotedly and individually <u>loves you just as you are.</u> . . . Accustom yourself to the wonderful thought that God loves you with a tenderness, a generosity, and an intimacy that surpasses all your dreams.

ABBE HENRI DE TOURVILLE

Contents

YOU ARE A PEARL
OF GREAT PRICE:

God's Unbelievable Investment in Us

MERCIFUL LOVE

GEORGE WHITEFIELD

Be mindful of your mercy, O Lord,
and of your steadfast love,
for they have been from of old.

PSALM 25:6 NRSV

25:12-14

"Who are those who fear the Lord? He will show them the path they should choose. They will live in prosperity and their children will inherit the land. The Lord is a friend to those who fear him. He teaches them his covenant."

Adam and Eve had eaten the fruit of which God had commanded them that they should not eat. When arraigned before God, they could not be brought to confess it. What reason can be given as to why the sentence of death should not be pronounced against the prisoners at the bar? How can God, consistently with His justice, possibly forgive them? Yet mercy cries: Spare these sinners, spare the work of Your own hands! Look then, wisdom contrives a scheme how God may be just and yet be merciful.

An amazing scene of divine love here opens to our view, which from all eternity had been hidden in the heart of God! Although Adam and Eve were repentant and did not so much as put up one single petition for pardon, God immediately passes sentence upon the serpent and reveals to them a Savior.

Adam and Eve stood by as criminals, and God could not indulge them because they had broken His covenant. God the Father and God the Son had entered into a covenant concerning the salvation of the elect from all eternity. The first Adam proved false. Therefore, to secure the second covenant from being broken, God puts it into the hands of the second Adam, the Lord from heaven. Adam after the Fall stood no longer as our representative. He and Eve were only private persons, as we are, and were only to lay hold on the declaration of mercy contained in this promise by faith.

Extreme Love — 11

LOVE AND THE SAINT'S REST

RICHARD BAXTER

Put me on trial, LORD, and cross-examine me.
Test my motives and my heart.
For I am always aware of your unfailing love,
and I have lived according to your truth.
→ PSALM 26:2–3 NLT

Christian, believe this and think on it: You shalt be eternally embraced in the arms of that love which was from everlasting and will extend to everlasting. You will be embraced by that love which brought the Son of God's love from heaven to earth, from earth to the cross, from the cross to the grave, from the grave to glory. You will be in the arms of that love which was weary, hungry, tempted, scorned, scourged, buffeted, spit upon, crucified, and pierced; which did fast, pray, teach, heal, weep, sweat, bleed, and die. It will be loving and rejoicing, not loving and sorrowing. Yes, it will make Satan's court ring with the news that the saints are arrived safe in the bosom of Christ, out of the reach of hell forever.

Know this, believer, to your everlasting comfort: If those arms have once embraced you, His love to you will not be as yours was on earth to Him—seldom and cold. He who would not cease nor abate His love for all your enmity, unkind neglects, and churlish resistances, can He cease to love you when He has made you truly lovely? He who keeps you so constant in your love to Him that you can challenge tribulation, distress, persecution, famine, nakedness, peril, or sword, how much more will He Himself be constant!

[Handwritten margin note, top left:] Thank you Jesus for cleansing my sins, for forgiving me, and for not giving up on me. Only in you can I confidently claim this Psalm of David.

[Handwritten note, bottom:] Accepting that I was created lovely by God is hard to accept sometimes. Truly lovely? How can that be when I fail so often?! I'm grateful that that loveliness is NOT me, but Jesus covering me and shining through me. I am wretched alone, but in Jesus I am truly lovely.

SPECIAL LOVE

CHARLES FINNEY

This is how God showed his love among us:
He sent his one and only Son into the world
that we might live through him.
1 JOHN 4:9 NIV

More is evidently implied in the expression "God so loved the world" than simply its greatness. It is most exceptional in its character. Unless we understand this, we shall be in danger of falling into the strange mistake of some people who are forever talking about God's love for sinners but whose notions of the nature of this love never lead to repentance or to holiness. Some people seem to think of this love as simply good nature. They conceive of God only as a very good-natured being, whom nobody needs to fear. Such notions have not the least influence toward holiness but the very opposite. It is only when we come to understand what this love is in its nature that we feel its moral power promoting holiness.

It may be reasonably asked, "If God so loved the world with a love characterized by only greatness, why did He not save all the world without sacrificing His Son?" This question suffices to show us that there is deep meaning in this word. It was not a mere emotion or feeling. It was not a blind impulse. God had emotion but not emotion only. Indeed the Bible everywhere teaches us that God's love for man, lost in his sins, was paternal—the love of a father for his offspring—in this case, for a rebellious, disobedient, prodigal offspring. In this love there must, of course, blend the deepest compassion.

LOVE AND TENDERNESS

HANNAH WHITALL SMITH

He redeems me from death and crowns me
with love and tender mercies.
PSALM 103:4 NLT

Discomfort and unrest are impossible to the souls who come to know that God is their real and actual Father. I must make it plain that it is a father: such as our highest instincts tell us a good father ought to be, of whom I am speaking. Sometimes earthly fathers are unkind or tyrannical or selfish or even cruel—or they are merely indifferent and neglectful—but none of these can be called good fathers. But God, who is good, must be a good father or not a father at all. We must all of us have known good fathers in this world or at least can imagine them. I knew one, and he filled my childhood with sunshine by his most lovely fatherhood. I have learned to know a little about the perfect fatherhood of God because of my experience with this lovely earthly father.

But God is not only a father, He is a mother as well, and we have all of us known mothers whose love and tenderness have been without bound or limit. And it is very certain that God could never have created earthly fathers and mothers who were more tender and more loving than He is Himself. We must heap together all the best of all the fathers and mothers we have ever known or can imagine, and we must tell ourselves that this is only a faint image of God, our Father in heaven. What a good father ought to do, God, who is our Father, is absolutely sure to do.

LOVE AND THE RAINBOW

JONATHAN EDWARDS

Like the appearance of a rainbow in a cloud on a rainy day,
so was the appearance of the brightness all around it.
This was the appearance of the likeness of
the glory of the LORD.
EZEKIEL 1:28 NKJV

Glory belongs to the Father and the Son: to the Father that He so loved the world that He gave His only begotten Son, to the Son that He so loved the world as to give up Himself. But there is equal glory due to the Holy Spirit for He is that love of the Father and the Son to the world. Just so much as the first two Persons of the Godhead glorify Themselves by showing the astonishing greatness of Their love and grace, just so much is that wonderful love and grace glorified by the Holy Spirit.

Christ purchased for us that we should have the favor of God and might enjoy His love, but this love is the Holy Spirit, which is but the indwelling of the Holy Spirit in the heart. Christ purchased for us spiritual joy and comfort, which is in a participation of God's joy and happiness, which joy and happiness is the Holy Spirit. The Holy Spirit is the sum of all good things.

The various sorts of rays of the sun and their beautiful colors do well represent the Spirit. They well represent the love and grace of God and were made use of for this purpose in the rainbow after the flood, and I suppose also in that rainbow that was seen round about the throne by Ezekiel, and round the head of Christ by John in Revelation 10:1.

THE BRIDEGROOM'S LOVE

GEORGE WHITEFIELD

God gave the land of these kings as an inheritance—
His faithful love endures forever.
PSALM 136:21 NLT

Do you desire one who can love you? None can love you like Christ. His love is incomprehensible; His love passes all other love. The love of the Lord Jesus is first and without beginning; His love is free without any motive; His love is great without any measure; His love is constant without any change; His love is everlasting.

The love of the Lord Jesus Christ brought Him down from heaven and veiled His divinity in a human soul and body. It was love that made Him subject to hunger, thirst, and sorrow. His love carried Him back to heaven that He might make intercession for those whom He had redeemed.

If you have promised yourself to Christ, you will converse with Him. You will endeavor to promote His interest and advance His name in the world.

It is likewise your folly to refuse and neglect the gracious gifts of being the spouse of Christ. You forfeit all love that He would bestow upon you. You choose rags before robes, rubbish before gold, pebbles before jewels, wounds before healing, defilement before cleansing, deformity before comeliness, trouble before peace, slavery before liberty, the service of the devil before the service of Christ. You choose dishonor before a crown, death before life, hell before heaven, eternal misery and torment before everlasting joy and glory.

Consider who the Lord Jesus is, whom you are invited to embrace yourselves with. There is none comparable to Jesus Christ.

LOVING THOUGHTS

Thomas Watson

I hate vain thoughts: but thy law do I love.
Psalm 119:113 KJV

A blessed sign of love is to entertain good thoughts of God. He who loves his friend construes what his friend does in the best sense. Malice interprets all in the worst sense; love interprets all in the best sense. Love is an excellent commentator upon divine guidance; it thinks no evil. He who loves God has a good opinion of God.

This is the language of a gracious spirit: "My God sees what a hard heart I have; therefore, He drives in one wedge of trial after another to break my heart. He knows how I am full of bad temper, how sick of a disease; therefore, He cleanses by blood to save my life. This severe action is either to restrain some vice or to exercise some grace. How good is God who will not let me alone in my sins but smites my body to save my soul!" In this way, he who loves God takes everything with a good attitude.

Love puts a glowing interpretation upon all of God's actions. You who are prone to murmur at God, as if He had dealt ill with you, be humbled for this. Say to yourself, "If I loved God more, I should have better thoughts of God." It is Satan who makes us have good thoughts of ourselves and hard thoughts of God. Love takes all in the fairest sense; it thinks no evil.

THE GREATEST THING

JEREMY TAYLOR

"Who is like you, O Lord, among the gods?
Who is like you, majestic in holiness,
awesome in splendor, doing wonders?"
EXODUS 15:11 NRSV

Love is the greatest thing that God can give us, and it is the greatest thing we can give to God. It is the old; it is the new; it is the great commandment; it is all the commandments. The consideration of God's goodness and bounty are most commonly the first motive of our love. But when we are once entered and have tasted the goodness of God, we love the source for its own excellence.

Perfection and admiration create love. For perfection and admiration, there is in God an infinite nature, unchanging, eternal, all-powerful, holy, merciful, just, and perfect. The consideration of which may be heightened if we consider our distance from all these glories: our smallness, limited nature, inconstancy, weakness, ignorance, poverty, harsh nature, and unmerciful inclinations.

Love does all things that may please the beloved person. Love is obedient. Love gives away all things to advance the interest of the beloved person. Love is always liberal and expressive. It suffers all things that are imposed by its beloved. Love is patient and content with anything, provided it can be with its beloved. Love is also impatient of anything that may displease the beloved. Love is not divided between God and God's enemy. We must love God with all our heart; that is, give Him a whole and undivided affection, having love for nothing else but such things which He allows and which He commands or loves Himself.

ABSOLUTE LOVE

ELIZABETH PRENTISS

*The LORD is good to those whose hope is in him,
to the one who seeks him; it is good to wait quietly
for the salvation of the LORD.*
LAMENTATIONS 3:25–26 NIV

Life is too precious to spend in a treadmill. Having been pardoned by your God and Savior, the next thing you have to do is to show your gratitude for this infinite favor by consecrating yourself entirely to Him, body, soul, and spirit. This is the least you can do. He has bought you with a price, and you are no longer your own. "But," you may reply, "this is contrary to my nature. I love my own way. I desire ease and pleasure; I desire to go to heaven, but I want to be carried there on a bed of flowers. Can I not give myself so far to God as to feel a sweet sense of peace with Him and be sure of final salvation, and yet, to a certain extent, indulge and gratify myself? If I give myself entirely away to Him and lose all ownership in myself, He may deny me many things I greatly desire. He may make my life hard and wearisome, depriving me of all that now makes it agreeable." But, I reply, this is no matter of parley and discussion; it is not optional with God's children whether they will pay Him a part of the price they owe Him and keep back the rest. He asks, and He has a right to ask, for all you have and all you are. And if you shrink from what is involved in such a surrender, you should fly to Him at once and never rest till He has conquered this secret disinclination to give to Him as freely and as fully as He has given to you. It is true that such an act of consecration on your part may involve a great deal of future discipline and correction. But as soon as you become the Lord's by your own deliberate and conscious act, He will begin that process of sanctification which is to make you holy as He is holy, perfect as He is perfect. He becomes at once your Physician as well as your dearest and best Friend, but He will use no painful remedy that can be avoided. Remember that it is His will that you should be sanctified and that the work of making you holy is His, not yours. At the same time you are not to sit with folded hands, waiting for this blessing. You are to avoid laying hindrances in His way, and you are to exercise faith in Him as just as able and just as willing to give you sanctification as He was to give you redemption.

LOVE AND THE NEW COVENANT

William Tyndale

"O Lord, God of Israel,
there is no God like you in heaven above or on earth beneath,
keeping covenant and steadfast love for your servants
who walk before you with all their heart."
1 Kings 8:23 NRSV

If anyone thinks he believes in Christ and has not the law written in his heart to love his brother as Christ loved him, the faith of that person is vain. It is built upon sand of his own imagination and not upon the rock of God's word. True faith makes a man to love his brother.

In the sacrifices of the Old Testament, Moses offered half the blood to God and sprinkled the people with the other half to confirm the covenant. The new covenant of Christ is confirmed with a better blood to make people see love and to love again. For if God gave us His Son, what will He deny us? If God so loved us when we were sinners and knew Him not, how much more does He love us now that we love again?

Our service to Christ is only to believe in Him for the remission of sin, to call upon Him and give Him thanks, and to love our neighbors for His sake. Now they who believe in Christ for the remission of their sins and for His sake love their foes are not Christ's enemies. Sin is forgiven only for Christ's sake; and again, that our duty is to love our neighbors no less than Christ loved us. Let us exhort each other to trust in Christ and to love each other as Christ did.

LOVE EVERLASTING

Charles Haddon Spurgeon

But the steadfast love of the Lord is
from everlasting to everlasting
on those who fear him.
Psalm 103:17 NRSV

Jesus will not let His people forget His love. If all the love they have enjoyed should be forgotten, He will visit them with fresh love. "Do you forget My cross?" says He. "I will cause you to remember it. At My table I will manifest Myself once more to you."

Mothers do not let their children forget them. If the boy has gone to Australia and does not write home, his mother writes, "Has John forgotten his mother?" Then there comes back a sweet letter, which proves that the gentle reminder was not in vain. So is it with Jesus. He says to us, "Remember Me." Our response is, "We will remember Your love."

Your love is ancient as the glory that You had with the Father before the world was. We remember Your eternal love when You embraced us. We remember the love that suggested the sacrifice of Yourself. We remember Your love as it was manifest to us in Your holy life, from the manger of Bethlehem to the garden of Gethsemane. We track You from the cradle to the grave—for every word and deed of Yours was love. We rejoice in Your love that death did not exhaust Your love that shone resplendently in Your resurrection. We remember that burning fire of love that will never let You hold Your peace until Your chosen ones are all safely housed, until Zion is glorified and Jerusalem settled on her everlasting foundations of light and love in heaven.

CHEERFUL LOVE

CHARLES HADDON SPURGEON

*Each of you must give as you have made up your mind,
not reluctantly or under compulsion,
for God loves a cheerful giver.*
2 CORINTHIANS 9:7 NRSV

If you know the love of Jesus as the deer thirsts for the brooks, so will you desire greater portions of His love. If you do not desire to know Him better, then you do not love Him because love always cries, "Nearer, nearer." Only be content with an increasing acquaintance with Jesus. Seek to know more of Him in His divine nature, in His human relationship, in His finished work, in His death, in His resurrection, in His present glorious intercession, and in His future royal appearance. An increase of love to Jesus and a better understanding of His love to us is one of the best tests of growth in grace.

Our God requires no slaves to adorn His throne. He is the Lord of the empire of love and would have His servants dressed in the uniform of joy. If He sees that we serve Him from force and not because we love Him, He will reject our offering. Take away joyful willingness from the Christian, and you have removed the test of his sincerity. In the joy of the Lord, we are strong.

Cheerfulness is to our service what oil is to the wheels of a railway car. Without oil, the axle soon grows hot and accidents occur. If there be not a cheerfulness to oil our wheels, our spirits will be clogged with weariness. Let us show to the people of the world that our religion is to us a delight and a joy!

COPY GOD'S LOVE

Thomas Watson

*"Whoever has my commands and keeps them
is the one who loves me.
The one who loves me will be loved by my Father,
and I too will love them and show myself to them."*
John 14:21 NIV

It is a vain thing to say we love Christ if we slight His commands. Does that child love his father who refuses to obey him? If we love God, we shall obey Him in things difficult and things dangerous.

Forgiving our enemies is hard. We are apt to forget kindnesses and remember injuries, but if we love God, we shall leave behind offenses. When we seriously consider how many affronts and provocations He has put up with at our hands, this makes us copy Him and endeavor to bury an injury than to retaliate it.

Love made Christ suffer for us. Love was the chain that fastened Him to the cross. If we love God, we shall be willing to suffer for Him. Love is the most suffering grace. It will suffer reproaches, bonds, and imprisonments for Christ's sake. Love will carry men out above their own strength. How did divine affection carry the early saints above the love of life and the fear of death! These divine heroes were willing to suffer rather than to make the name of God suffer by their cowardice. They refused to come out of prison on sinful terms.

Many will not forego the least comfort or undergo the least cross for His sake. May not Christ suspect us when we pretend to love Him and yet will endure nothing for Him?

LOVE IN NATURE AND IN GOD'S WORD

ELLEN G. WHITE

I will sing of your love and justice, LORD.
I will praise you with songs.
PSALM 101:1 NLT

The poet and the naturalist have many things to say about nature, but the Christian enjoys the beauty of the earth with the highest appreciation. The Christian recognizes His Father's handiwork and perceives His love in flower and shrub and tree. No one can fully appreciate the significance of hill and vale, river and sea who does not look upon them as an expression of God's love to man.

God speaks to us through His thoughtful workings and through the influence of His Spirit upon the heart. In our circumstances and surroundings, in the changes daily taking place around us, we may find precious lessons if our hearts are but open to discern them.

God speaks to us in His Word. Here we have in clearer lines the revelation of His character, His dealings with men, and the great work of redemption. Here is open before us the history of patriarchs and prophets and other holy men of old. We see how they struggled through discouragement like our own, how they fell under temptation as we have done and yet took heart again and conquered through the grace of God—and we are encouraged in our striving after righteousness.

As we read of the precious experiences granted them, the light and love and blessing it was theirs to enjoy, and the work they wrought through the grace given them, the Spirit that inspired them kindles in our hearts a desire to be like them in character—like them to walk with God.

THE PATH OF LOVE

WILLIAM TYNDALE

All the paths of the Lord are steadfast love and faithfulness,
for those who keep his covenant and his decrees.
PSALM 25:10 NRSV

By faith we receive the love of God, and by love we give it out again. We must do so freely, after the example of Christ and without any other motive save our neighbor's benefit. We must bestow pure love ourselves—all that we have and all that we are able to do, even on our enemies to bring them to God.

Christ did not do His deeds to obtain heaven. Heaven was His already. He did them freely for our sakes and to bring the favor of God to us and us to God. No natural son does his father's will because he would be heir. He is already heir by birth. His father gave him that out of pure love before he was born. Servants work for hire, children for love. So a Christian acts freely, considering nothing but the will of God and the value he can give his neighbor.

A gentle pastor, Jesus brings the Spirit of God, which loosens the bonds of Satan and couples us to God and His will through strong faith and fervent love. The poor and wretched sinner feels so great mercy, love, and kindness in God that he is sure in himself that it is not possible for God to forsake him or withdraw His mercy and love. He boldly cries out with Paul, saying, "Who shall separate us from the love that God loves us with?" In all tribulations, a Christian perceives that God is His Father and loves him even as he loved Christ.

LOVE IN THREE WORDS

REUBEN ARCHER TORREY

Whoever does not love does not know God,
because God is love.
1 JOHN 4:8 NIV

My subject is the greatest sentence that was ever written. That sentence is in the Bible. The Bible has a way of putting more in a single sentence than other writers can put in a whole book. This sentence has in it but three words: God is love. Each word is a monosyllable. One word has four letters, one three, and one only two. Yet these nine letters, forming three monosyllables, contain so much truth that the world has been pondering it for centuries and has not gotten to the bottom of it yet.

"God is love" is the greatest sentence ever written. It sums up the whole contents of the Bible. If I were asked for a sentence to print in letters of gold on the outside of our Bible, a sentence that summed up the whole contents of the Book, it would be this one: "God is love." It is the subject of the first chapter of Genesis, it is the subject of the last chapter of Revelation, and it is the subject of every chapter that lies in between.

The Bible is simply God's love story, the story of the love of a holy God to a sinful world. There is mighty power in that one short sentence, power to break the hardest heart, power to reach individual men and women who are sunk down in sin and to lift them up until they are fit for a place beside the Lord Jesus Christ upon the throne.

FIRST LOVE, LAST LOVE

CHARLES HADDON SPURGEON

"I know your deeds, your love and faith,
your service and perseverance,
and that you are now doing more than you did at first."
REVELATION 2:19 NIV

Look back through all of your experiences and think of the ways that the Lord your God has led you and how He has fed and clothed you every day. He has borne with your ill manners. He has put up with all your murmurings and all your longings after sensual pleasures. He has supplied you with spiritual nourishment from heaven. Think of how His grace has been sufficient for you in all your troubles. His blood has been a pardon to you in all your sins. His rod and His staff have comforted you.

When you have looked back upon the love of the Lord, then let faith survey His love in the future, for remember that Christ's covenant and blood have something more in them than the past. He who has loved you and pardoned you shall never cease to love and pardon. He is alpha, and He shall be omega, also. He is first, and He shall be last. When you shall stand in the cold floods of Jordan, you need not fear because death cannot separate you from His love. Now, soul, is not your love refreshed? Does not this make you love Jesus? Does not a flight through limitless plains of His love inflame your heart and compel you to delight yourself in the Lord your God? Surely as we meditate on the love of the Lord, our hearts burn within us, and we long to love Him more.

GIFTS OF LOVE

Reuben Archer Torrey

See what great love the Father has lavished on us,
that we should be called children of God!
1 John 3:1 niv

God shows His love by His gifts. Suppose on his coronation day, King Edward, after all the ceremonies were over, had taken his carriage and had ridden down to the East End of London and had seen some ragged, wretched boy. Suppose his great heart of love had gone out to that boy, and stepping up to that poor wanderer, he had said: "I love you, and I am going to take you in my carriage to the palace. I am going to dress you fit to be a king's son, and you shall be known as the son of King Edward the Seventh." Would it not have been wonderful? But it would not have been as wonderful as that the infinitely holy God should have looked down upon you and me in our filthiness and rags and depravity, and that He should have so loved us that He should have bestowed upon us to be called the sons of God.

I have a friend in the university. We thought a good deal of each other, but I did not know how much he loved me. Years after, he learned that I was in a position in which I needed fifteen hundred dollars. The next day he came to me. "Let me give you that fifteen hundred dollars! You can pay it back later."

He gave me that fifteen hundred dollars, and I have paid it back, but he did not know I would. I knew then that man loved me.

LOVE AND THE DARK SHADOW

Ellen G. White

Unto the upright there ariseth light in the darkness:
he is gracious, and full of compassion, and righteous.
Psalm 112:4 kjv

God has bound our hearts to Him by unnumbered gifts in heaven and on earth. Through the things of nature, He has sought to reveal Himself to us. Yet these but imperfectly represent His love. Although all these evidences have been given, the enemy of good blinded the minds of men so that they looked upon God with fear. They thought of Him as severe and unforgiving. Satan led men to conceive of God as one who is a severe judge, a harsh and exacting creditor. He pictured the Creator as a being who is watching with jealous eye to discern the errors and mistakes of men so that He may visit judgments upon them.

It was to remove this dark shadow by revealing to the world the infinite love of God that Jesus came to live among men. He went about doing good and healing all who were oppressed by Satan. There were whole villages where there was not a moan of sickness in any house, for He had passed through them and healed all their sick. His work gave evidence of His divine anointing. Love, mercy, and compassion were revealed in every act of His life. His heart went out in tender sympathy to the children of men. He took man's nature so that He might reach man's wants. The poorest and humblest were not afraid to approach Him. Even little children were attracted to Him. They loved to climb upon His knees and gaze into the pensive face, compassionate with love.

BESET WITH LOVE

Hannah Whitall Smith

Thou hast beset me behind and before,
and laid thine hand upon me.
Psalm 139:5 KJV

We are told in our Psalm that God besets our path. Some of us know what it is to be intruded upon by unwelcome and unpleasant people. Perhaps we never have thought that God besets us. He loves us so that He cannot leave us alone. Neither coldness nor rebuffs on our part can drive Him away. Yes, it is gloriously true!

Moreover, He besets us behind as well as before, just as a mother does. She goes after her children and picks up all they have dropped and clears away all the litter they have left behind them. We mothers begin this in the nursery with the blocks and playthings, and we go on with it all our lives long. We are seeking continually to set straight that which our children have left crooked behind them. Often it is at the cost of much toil and trouble, but always with a love that makes the toil and trouble nothing in comparison to caring for the children we love.

What good mother ever turned away the poor little tearful darling who came with a tangled knot for her unraveling or refused to help the eager, rosy boy to unwind his kite strings? Suppose it has been their own fault that the knots and tangles have come; still her love can sympathize with and pity the very faults themselves. All this and more does our God do for us from our earliest infancy, long even before we know enough to be conscious of it, until the very end of our earthly lives.

LOVE ACROSS THE AGES

CHARLES FINNEY

For God so loved the world,
that he gave his only begotten Son,
that whosoever believeth in him should not perish,
but have everlasting life.
JOHN 3:16 KJV

Long before He formed a moral universe, He knew perfectly what it must cost Him to redeem sinners, and He knew that the result would amply justify all the cost. He knew that a wonder of mercy would be wrought—that the suffering demanded of Christ, great as it was, would be endured—and that results infinitely glorious would accrue therefrom.

He looked down the track of time into the distant ages—where there might be seen the joys of redeemed saints, who are singing their songs and striking their harps anew with the everlasting song, and was not this enough for the heart of infinite love to enjoy?

When you come to see Him face-to-face and tell Him what you think of it—when you are some thousands of years older than you are now—will you not adore that wisdom that manages this scheme, and the infinite love in which it had its birth?

God wants volunteers to help on this great work. God has given Himself, and given His Son, and sent His Spirit. More laborers still are needed. What will you give? Say not, "I have nothing to give." You can give yourself—your eyes, your ears, your hands, your mind, your heart, all. How many young men are ready to go? And how many young women? Whose heart leaps up, crying, "Here am I! Send me!"?

MARVELOUS LOVE

F. B. Meyer

So thank God for his marvelous love,
for his miracle mercy to the children he loves.
Psalm 107:21 msg

Great and marvelous are Your works, God, that our soul knows quite well. You have showed marvelous loving-kindness. We must sing to You because You have done marvelous things. It is marvelous that You have set Your love upon us, that You have watched over our interests with un-wearied care, that our sins or unbelief have never diverted Your love from us.

"Marvelous" is the only word we can use as we think of the well-beloved Son who descended to the bed in a manger, of the agony and bloody sweat of the cross and passion—and all for us who were His enemies. But it is most marvelous of all that You made us children and joint heirs with Christ. To think that we shall shine as the sun in Your kingdom and be included in that circle of love and life of which the throne of God and the Lamb is the center! Surely the marvels of Your grace will only seem the greater when eternity with its boundless ages gives us time to explore them.

The danger, however, is that we should become strong in our own conceit and credit ourselves with the position which is due to the grace of God alone. We need the truly humble spirit of the little child that we may never boast of ourselves! God cannot trust some of us with prosperity and success because our nature could not stand them.

BLESSINGS OF LOVE

HUDSON TAYLOR

You bestow on him blessings forever;
you make him glad with the joy of your presence.
PSALM 21:6 NRSV

We frequently use the word "blessing" so vaguely as to overlook the primary meaning. For instance, we use it frequently as a synonym of praise. In speaking of blessing God, we think of praising Him. Blessing does not merely mean praise. Blessing is the moving of the heart toward an object of affection.

Blessing is always accompanied with joy. It is a joy, and it gives joy both to the giver and the receiver. A little child playing with his toys may be both happy and satisfied. But the little one hears the mother's footsteps, sees the mother open the door, and instantly the toys are dropped and forgotten. The little arms are stretched out and the little feet are running to meet the welcome mother. The motherly arms are as quickly stretched forth toward the child, and with longer steps the mother hastens to meet the little one and clasps the child to her bosom.

But whose heart is the gladder? The little one's heart is full. The mother's heart is also full; but her capacity is greater, and so her joy is deeper. And is not this true of our heavenly Father? When His heart blesses ours and ours blesses Him, we are full of joy. But His heart is infinitely greater than ours, and His joy in His people far exceeds all their joy in Him as the infinite exceeds the finite.

JESUS' GIFT OF LOVE

ANDREW MURRAY

Christ loved the church and gave himself up for her.
EPHESIANS 5:25 NRSV

So great and wonderful was the love of Jesus toward us that He actually gave Himself for us and to us. The one thing that is necessary is that we should rightly understand and firmly believe His surrender for us. Yes, Jesus gives Himself to prepare for Himself a pure people, a people of His own, and a zealous people. When I receive Him, when I believe that He gave Himself to do this for me, I shall certainly experience it. I shall be purified through Him, shall be held fast as His possession, and shall be filled with zeal and joy to work for Him.

The more I understand and contemplate Jesus' surrender of Himself for me, the more I give myself again to Him. The surrender is a mutual one. The love comes from both sides. His giving of Himself makes such an impression on my heart that my heart with the same love and joy becomes entirely His. I know that I have Jesus wholly for me and that He has me wholly for Him.

Through faith I live in Jesus who loved me and gave Himself for me. And I say, "No longer do I live, but Christ liveth in me." In His great love, the Father gave the Son. It was out of love that Jesus gave Himself. The taking, the having of Jesus is the entrance to a life in the love of God: this is the highest life. Through faith we must press into love and dwell there.

LOVE AND DUTY

Reuben Archer Torrey

And walk in love, as Christ also hath loved us,
and hath given himself
for us an offering and a sacrifice to God
for a sweetsmelling savour.
Ephesians 5:2 KJV

I once heard a story that brought me such a glimpse of God's love as I never had before. I do not know whether it is true or not. A man was set to watch a railway drawbridge over a river. He threw it open and let vessels through. He heard the whistle of a train up the track and sprang to the lever to bring the bridge back into place. As he was doing so, he accidentally pushed his boy into the river. He heard the boy cry, "Father, save me; I am drowning." What should he do? The man stood at the post of duty and brought the bridge back so that the train could pass over in safety. Then he jumped into the river to save his boy, but it was too late. He sacrificed his boy to do his duty.

When I heard that story, I wondered if it had been my boy what I would have done. That man owed it to those on the train to do what he did. God owed you and me nothing. We were guilty rebels against Him.

What are you going to do with His love? Accept it, or trample it underfoot? Accept Christ, and you accept that love. Reject Christ, and you trample that love underfoot. I cannot understand how any man or woman in their right senses can harden their hearts against the love of God.

GOD'S GIFT OF LOVE

Andrew Murray

Jesus said to them,
"If God were your Father, you would love me,
for I came from God and now I am here.
I did not come
on my own, but he sent me."
John 8:42 NRSV

This is the love of God, not that He gives us something, but that He gives us someone in whom is all life and blessing—Jesus Himself. It is the will of the Father that we should have Jesus as ours, even as He has Him. God has given His Son, given Him wholly to become ours.

How I do wish that all Christians may understand this. The one great work of God's love for us is that He gives us His Son. In Him, we have all. The one great work of our heart must be to receive Jesus who has been given to us and to consider Him and use Him as ours. I must begin every day anew with the thought, *I have Jesus to do all for me.* In all weakness, darkness, or danger, and in the case of every desire or need, let your first thought always be, *I have Jesus to make everything right for me because God has given Him to me.* Let this always be your first thought: *The Father has given me Jesus to care for me.*

For this purpose, consider this gift of God every day as yours. Take Him new every day. Through faith, you have the Son. The love of God has given the Son. Take Him and hold Him fast in the love of your heart.

LOVE FROM A HEIGHT

REUBEN ARCHER TORREY

He will send from heaven and save me,
he will put to shame those who trample on me.
God will send forth his steadfast love and his faithfulness.
PSALM 57:3 NRSV

God shows His love by the sacrifice He has made for us. Sacrifice is the great test of love. People tell you that they love you, but you cannot tell whether they really love you until the opportunity comes for them to make a sacrifice for you.

You and I sometimes dwell upon the love of Christ to give up heaven for us. We look at Him in the courtyard of Pilate, fastened to the whipping post with His bare back exposed to the lash of the Roman soldier. We look at Him as the lash cuts into His back again, again, and again until it is all torn and bleeding. Oh, how He loves us!

But looking down from the throne in heaven was God, and every lash that cut the back of Christ cut the heart of God. We see the soldiers with the crown of thorns, pressing it on His brow, and we see the blood flowing down. Oh, how He loved us! But every thorn that pierced His brow pierced also the heart of God. Through that awful day we see Him on the cross. We hear the last cry. We see how He loved us. But looking down from the throne of light and glory was God, and every nail that pierced His hands and feet pierced the heart of God.

What are you going to do about this love?

Because You're Worth It:

Getting Over Our Inferiority Complex

LOVE AND SALVATION

J. C. RYLE

May those who long for your saving help always say,
"The LORD is great!"
PSALM 40:16 NIV

William you say that you are afraid to come to God? Your fear is needless. You shall not be cast out, if you will but come in the way of faith in Christ. Our God is not an austere man. Our Father in heaven is full of mercy, love, and grace. I yield to none in desire to promote the love, mercy, and tenderness of God the Father.

We know that God is holy. We know He is just. We believe that He can be angry with them who go on still in sin. But we also believe that to those who draw near to Him in Christ Jesus, He is most merciful, most loving, most tender, and most compassionate. We tell you that the cross of Jesus Christ was the result and consequence of that love.

The cross was not the cause and reason of God's mercy but the result and consequence of the everlasting love of God the Father, God the Son, and God the Holy Ghost toward a poor, lost, and bankrupt world. Draw near in faith by that living way, Christ Jesus to the Father. Think not for a moment that in drawing near to God the Father by Christ, God the Father will not receive you. He will receive you gladly. As the father did to the prodigal son when he ran to meet him—fell on his neck and kissed him—so will God the Father do to that soul who draws near to Him in the name of Christ.

BELOVED FRIEND

THOMAS WATSON

His mouth is most sweet;
Yea, he is altogether lovely.
This is my beloved, and this is my friend,
O daughters of Jerusalem.
SONG OF SOLOMON 5:16 ASV

The words "your God" imply the relation of a friend. A friend is, as Saint Augustine says, half one's self. He is studious and desirous how he may do his friend good. He promotes his welfare as his own. Jonathan ventured the king's displeasure for his friend David. God is our friend; therefore, He will turn all things to our good. There are false friends. Christ was betrayed by a friend. But God is the best friend.

God is a faithful friend. He is faithful in His love. He gave His very heart to us when He gave the Son out of His bosom. Here was a pattern of love without a parallel. He is faithful in His promises. He is faithful in His dealings.

God is a permanent friend. Friends often fail at a pinch. Many deal with their friends as women do with flowers; while they are fresh, they put them in their bosoms, but when they begin to wither they throw them away. Accordingly, if prosperity shines on men then friends will look upon them. But if there be a cloud of adversity on them, they will not come near them. But God is a friend forever. Although David walked in the shadow of death, he knew he had a friend by him. God, being such a friend, will make all things work for our good. A friend will seek the good of his friend. God never takes off His love wholly from His people.

LIGHTEN YOUR LOAD

HANNAH WHITALL SMITH

Praise be to the Lord, to God our Savior,
who daily bears our burdens.
Our God is a God who saves;
from the Sovereign LORD comes escape from death.
PSALM 68:19–20 NIV

Most Christians are like a man who was toiling along the road, bending under a heavy burden, when a wagon overtook him and the driver kindly offered to help him on his journey. He joyfully accepted the offer but, when seated in the wagon, continued to bend beneath his burden, which he still kept on his shoulders.

"Why do you not lay down your burden?" asked the kindhearted driver.

"Oh!" replied the man. "I feel that it is almost too much to ask you to carry me, and I could not think of letting you carry my burden, too."

And so Christians who have given themselves into the care and keeping of the Lord Jesus still continue to bend beneath the weight of their burdens and often go weary and heavy-laden throughout the whole length of their journey. . . .

It is generally much less difficult for us to commit the keeping of our future to the Lord than it is to commit our present. We know we are helpless as regards the future, but we feel as if the present is in our own hands and must be carried on our own shoulders; and most of us have an unconfessed idea that it is a great deal to ask the Lord to carry ourselves and that we cannot think of asking Him to carry our burdens, too. . . .

[But] He made you, and therefore He understands you and knows how to manage you. You must trust Him to do it. Say to Him, "Here, Lord, I abandon myself to You. I have tried in every way I could think of to manage myself and to make myself what I know I ought to be, but I have always failed. Now I give it up to You. Take entire possession of me. Work in me all the good pleasure of Your will. Mold and fashion me into such a vessel as seems good to You. I leave myself in Your hands, and I believe You will, according to Your promise, make me into a vessel unto Your own honor, 'sanctified, and meet for the Master's use, and prepared unto every good work.'" And here you must rest, trusting yourself to Him, continually and absolutely.

AMAZING LOVE

GEORGE WHITEFIELD

The amazing grace of the Master, Jesus Christ,
the extravagant love of God,
the intimate friendship of the Holy Spirit,
be with all of you.
2 CORINTHIANS 13:14 MSG

How do you and I wish we had known Jesus sooner and that we had more of His love? It is amazing love, it is forgiving love, it is dying love, it is exalted and interceding love, and it is glorified love. I am talking of the love of Jesus Christ who loved me before I loved Him. He saw me polluted in blood, full of sores, a slave to sin, death, and hell, running to destruction. Then He said unto my soul, "Live." He snatched me as a brand plucked from the burning. It was love that saved me. It was all of the free grace of God and that only.

My brethren, the kingdom of God is within me, and this fills me so full of love that I would not be in my natural state again, not for millions of millions of worlds. Eternity itself will be too short to set forth the love of the Lord Jesus Christ.

If there are any here who are strangers to this love of the Lord Jesus Christ, do not despair. Come, come unto Christ, and He will have mercy upon you. He will pardon all your sins. He will love you freely and take you to be with Himself. You need not fear, you need not despair when God has had mercy upon such a wretch as I. And He will save you also if you will come unto Him by faith.

LOVE AND JOY

Richard Baxter

"Rejoice in that day and leap for joy!
For indeed your reward is great in heaven."
Luke 6:23 NKJV

Infinite love must be a mystery to our finite capacity. The saints' everlasting rest must consist in the enjoyment of God by love. Joy has a share in this attainment of the inconceivable comfort that the blessed feel in seeing, knowing, loving, and being beloved of God. All Christ's ways of mercy tend to end in the saints' joys. He wept, sorrowed, and suffered that they might rejoice. He sends the Spirit to be our comforter. He multiplies promises and makes known our future happiness that our joy may be full.

He never brings us into so low a condition that He does not leave us more cause of joy than sorrow. The Lord cares for our comfort here. What that joy will be where the soul has been perfectly prepared for joy! It shall be our work, our business, eternally to rejoice!

Poor, humble, drooping soul, how would it fill you with joy now, if a voice from heaven should tell you of the love of God, the pardon of your sins, and assure you of your part in these heavenly joys? What then will your joy be when your actual possession shall convince you of your title, and you shall be in heaven before you are well aware! It is not your joy only. It is a mutual joy as well as a mutual love. There is joy in heaven at your conversion, and there will be joy at your glorification. The angels will welcome you to heaven and congratulate your safe arrival.

CLAIM GOD'S LOVE

Hannah Whitall Smith

They that be whole need not a physician,
but they that are sick.
Matthew 9:12 KJV

Have you never tasted the luxury of indulging in hard thoughts against those who have, as you think, injured you? What a positive fascination it is to brood over their unkindness, to pry into their malice, and to imagine all sorts of wrong things about them. It has made you wretched, of course, but it has been a fascinating sort of wretchedness that you could not easily give up.

Like this is the luxury of doubting. Things have gone wrong with you in your experience. What is more natural than to conclude that for some reason God has forsaken you and does not love you? How irresistible is the conviction that you are too wicked for Him to care for or too difficult for Him to manage. You do not mean to blame Him or accuse Him of injustice, for you feel that His indifference toward you is fully deserved because of your unworthiness. This very ploy leaves you at liberty to indulge in your doubts under the guise of a just and true recognition of your own shortcomings.

The poor little lamb that has wandered from the flock and gotten lost in the wilderness might as well say, "The shepherd does not love me nor care for me nor remember me because I am lost. He only loves and cares for the lambs that never wander." But Jesus says He came not to save the righteous but sinners. Your very sinfulness and unworthiness is your chief claim upon His love and His care.

HOME FILLED WITH LOVE

Hannah Whitall Smith

Let him lead me to the banquet hall,
and let his banner over me be love.
Song of Solomon 2:4 niv

I was visiting once in a wealthy house, where there was an adopted girl upon whom was lavished all the love and tenderness and care that human hearts could give. And as I watched that child running about, free and lighthearted with the happy carelessness of childhood, I thought what a picture it was of our wonderful position as children in the house of our heavenly Father. And I said to myself, "Nothing could so grieve and wound the loving hearts around her as to see this little child beginning to be worried or anxious about herself in any way, about whether her food and clothes would be provided for her, or how she was to get her education or her future support. How much more must the great, loving heart of our God and Father be grieved and wounded at seeing His children taking so much anxious care and thought!" And I understood why it was that our Lord had said to us so emphatically, "Take no thought for yourselves."

Who is the best cared for in every household? It is the little children. And the least of all, the helpless baby receives the largest share. As I have read, the baby toils not, neither does he spin, and yet he is fed and clothed and loved and rejoiced in (Matthew 6:28 kjv).

Let the ways of childish confidence and freedom from care, which so please you and win your hearts in your own little ones, teach you what should be your ways with God.

LOVE WITHOUT BONDAGE

Charles Finney

But it was because the LORD loved you. . .
that he. . .redeemed you from the land of slavery.
Deuteronomy 7:8 NIV

God sought, in commending His love to us, to subdue our slavish fear. Someone said, "When I was young, I was conscious of fearing God, but I knew I did not love Him. The instruction I received led me to fear but not to love." So long as we think of God only as one to be feared, not to be loved, there will be a prejudice against Him as more an enemy than a friend.

Every sinner sees plainly that God must have good reason to be displeased with him. The selfish sinner judges God from himself. Knowing how he should feel toward one who had wronged him, he unconsciously infers that God must feel the same way toward every sinner. When he tries to pray, his heart won't; it is nothing but terror. He feels no attraction toward God, no real love.

God would lead us to serve Him in love and not in bondage. He would draw us forth into the liberty of the sons of God. He loves to see the obedience of the heart. He would inspire love enough to make all our service free, cheerful, and full of joy. If you wish to make others love you, you must give them your love. In this way God commends His love toward us in order to win our hearts to Himself and get us ready and fit to dwell forever in His eternal home.

LOVE BEYOND REASON

HENRY DRUMMOND

The LORD is slow to anger,
abounding in love
and forgiving sin and rebellion.
NUMBERS 14:18 NIV

A student went to a professor of theology and asked him how long it took him to understand the atonement, the love and forgiveness of God. The professor thought a moment and looked him in the face. "Eternity," he said. "Eternity, and I shall not understand it then."

God's love—how could we understand? God's forgiveness—how could we understand? We need not be distressed if we do not understand them. Most things in religion are matters of simple faith. But when we come to the atonement, we want to see through it and understand it—as if it were finite like ourselves, as if it could ever be compassed by our narrow minds—as if God did not know that we never could fathom it when He said "Believe it," instead of "Understand it."

We are not rationalists when we come to the love of God, or to faith or to prayer. We do not ask for a theory of love before we begin to love or a theory of prayer before we begin to pray. We just begin. When they brought the sick man once to Jesus, He just said, "Man, your sins are forgiven you," and the man just believed it. He did not ask, "But why should You forgive me?" The fact is, if we would come to Christ just now, we should never ask any questions. If you will not receive salvation as a fact, receive the Lord Jesus Christ as a gift.

THE LOVING FATHER

HANNAH WHITALL SMITH

I will be a father to him, and he shall be a son to me.
I will not take my steadfast love from him.
1 CHRONICLES 17:13 NRSV

In our Lord's last prayer (John 17:1), He says that He has declared to us the name of the Father so we may discover the wonderful fact that the Father loves us as He loved His Son. Now which one of us really believes this? We have read this chapter, I suppose, more often than almost any other chapter in the Bible. Yet do any of us believe that it is an actual, tangible fact that God loves us as much as He loved Christ? If we believed this to be the case, could we ever have an anxious or rebellious thought again? We would be absolutely and utterly sure always, under every conceivable circumstance, that the divine Father who loves us just as much as He loved His only begotten Son would care for us in the best possible way. He could tell us emphatically not to be anxious about anything because He knew His Father and knew that it was safe to trust Him completely.

"Your heavenly Father," Jesus says, "cares for the sparrows and the lilies, and of course therefore He will care for you who are of so much more value than many sparrows." How supremely foolish it is for us to be worried about things, when Christ has said that our heavenly Father knows that we have need of all these things! For being a good Father, He must in the very nature of the case supply it, when He knows our need.

STOLEN LOVE

ELLEN G. WHITE

For our gospel came not unto you in word only,
but also in power, and in the Holy Ghost,
and in much assurance.
1 THESSALONIANS 1:5 KJV

Some people seem to feel that they must be on probation and must prove to the Lord that they are reformed before they can claim His blessing. But they may claim the blessing of God even now. Jesus loves to have us come to Him just as we are—sinful, helpless, and dependent. We may come with all our weakness, our folly, our sinfulness, and fall at His feet. It is His glory to encircle us in the arms of His love and cleanse us from all impurity.

Here is where thousands fail. They do not believe that Jesus pardons them personally, individually. They do not take God at His Word. It is the privilege of all who comply with the conditions to know for themselves that pardon is freely extended for every sin. Put away the suspicion that God's promises are not meant for you. They are for every repentant transgressor. God does not deal with us as finite men deal with one another. His thoughts are thoughts of mercy, love, and tenderest compassion.

Satan is ready to steal away the blessed assurances of God. He desires to take every glimmer of hope and every ray of light from the soul, but you must not permit him to do this. Can you believe that when the poor sinner longs to return, longs to forsake his sins, the Lord sternly withholds him from coming to His feet in repentance? Away with such thoughts! He hates sin, but He loves the sinner.

LISTEN TO LOVE

Ellen G. White

Then a cloud appeared and covered them,
and a voice came from the cloud:
"This is my Son, whom I love. Listen to him!"
Mark 9:7 NIV

If we will but listen, God's created works will teach us precious lessons of obedience and trust. From the stars in their trackless courses through space down to the minutest atom, the things of nature obey the Creator's will. And God cares for everything and sustains everything that He has created. He who upholds the unnumbered worlds at the same time cares for the wants of the little brown sparrow that sings its humble song.

When the rich man feasts in his palace or when the poor man gathers his children about the scanty table, each is tenderly watched by the heavenly Father. No tears are shed that God does not notice. If we would but fully believe this, all undue anxieties would be dismissed. Our lives would not be so filled with disappointment as now. Everything, whether great or small, would be left in the hands of God, who is not perplexed by the multiplicity of cares or overwhelmed by their weight. We should then enjoy a rest of soul to which many have long been strangers.

As your senses delight in the attractive loveliness of the earth, think of the world that is to come that shall never know the blight of sin and death, where the face of nature will no more wear the shadow of the curse. Let your imagination picture the home of the saved, and remember that it will be more glorious than your brightest imagination can portray.

GOD'S LOVE IS ENOUGH

Hannah Whitall Smith

O Israel, hope in the LORD;
for with the LORD there is unfailing love.
His redemption overflows.
Psalm 130:7 nlt

Paul could say triumphantly in the midst of many and grievous trials that nothing could separate us from the love of God, which is in Christ Jesus our Lord. In the face of all we know about the God of all comfort, you can realize with Job, David, Paul, and the saints of all ages that nothing else is needed to quiet all your fears but just this: that God is. Nothing can separate you from His love, absolutely nothing—neither death nor life, nor angels, nor principalities, nor powers, nor things present, nor things to come, nor height, nor depth, nor any other creature. Every possible contingency is provided for here. Not one of them can separate you from the love of God, which is in Christ Jesus our Lord.

After such a declaration as this, how can any of us dare to question or doubt God's love? Since He loves us, He cannot exist and fail to help us. We know by our own experience what a necessity it is for love to pour itself out in blessing on the ones it loves. Can we not understand that God who is love, who is, if I may say so, made out of love, simply cannot help blessing us? We do not need to beg Him to bless us; He simply cannot help it.

Therefore God is enough! God is enough for time. God is enough for eternity. God is enough!

THE GOD OF COMFORT

HANNAH WHITALL SMITH

Let your steadfast love become my comfort
according to your promise to your servant.
PSALM 119:76 NRSV

Among all the names that reveal God, the "God of all comfort" seems to me one of the loveliest and the most absolutely comforting. The words "all comfort" admit of no limitation and no deductions. But it often seems that a large number of the children of God are full not of comfort but of the utmost discomfort. This discomfort arises from anxiety as to their relationship to God and doubts as to His love. They torment themselves with the thought that they are too good-for-nothing to be worthy of His care, and they suspect Him of being indifferent to their trials and of forsaking them in times of need. They are anxious and troubled by their indifference to the Bible, lack of fervency in prayer, and coldness of heart. They are tormented with regrets over their past and with anxieties for their future.

They feel unworthy to enter God's presence and dare not believe that they belong to Him. They can be happy and comfortable with their earthly friends, but they cannot be happy or comfortable with God. And although He declares Himself to be the God of all comfort, they continually complain that they cannot find comfort anywhere. Their sorrowful looks and the doleful tones of their voices show that they are speaking the truth.

Such Christians spread gloom and discomfort around them wherever they go. And the manifestly uncomfortable religious lives of so many Christians is, I am very much afraid, responsible for a large part of the unbelief of the world.

THE HEAVENLY FATHER'S LOVE

HUDSON TAYLOR

The LORD bless thee, and keep thee:
The LORD make his face shine upon thee,
and be gracious unto thee: The LORD lift up his
countenance upon thee, and give thee peace.
NUMBERS 6:24–26 KJV

We have dwelt upon the meaning of blessing, the moving of the heart toward an object of affection and contentment, and noticed that when love overflows, loving words, loving embraces, or loving gifts instinctively follow.

Considered as a father's blessing, could anything be more appropriate than "The Lord bless you and keep you"? Is not this just what every loving father seeks to do, to bless and keep his children? He does not find it an unwelcome task but his greatest delight.

Nor may we confine ourselves to paternal love in thinking of this subject. Rather take it as embracing also the love of the mother. We all know how the mother love delights to lavish itself on the objects of its care. With a patience that never tires, an endurance almost inexhaustible, and a care all but unlimited, how often has the mother sacrificed her very life for the welfare of her babe. But strong as is a mother's love, it may fail. God's love never fails.

"Jehovah, the Father, bless you and keep you." It is an individual blessing, and it includes every form of blessing, temporal as well as spiritual. He wants us, His children, to know and to enjoy the love that is the source of all blessing, the love that can never by finite words express its fullness, the love that eternal ages will never exhaust!

LOVE BEYOND LAW

Hannah Whitall Smith

"You have loved righteousness and hated wickedness;
therefore God, your God,
has set you above your companions
by anointing you with the oil of joy."
HEBREWS 1:9 NIV

The scriptures reveal to us glimpses of the delight, satisfaction, and joy our Lord has in us. That we should need Him is easy to comprehend; that He should need us seems incomprehensible. That our desire should be toward Him is a matter of course, but that His desire should be toward us passes the bounds of human belief. And yet over and over He says it, and what can we do but believe Him?

At every heart He is continually knocking and asking to be taken in as the supreme object of love. In a thousand ways He makes this offer of oneness with Himself to every believer. But all do not say, "Yes," to Him. Other loves and other interests seem to them too precious to be cast aside. They miss an unspeakable joy.

You, however, are not one of these. From the very first, eagerly and gladly to all His offers your soul has cried out, "Yes, Lord, yes!" What to them is lawful, love has made unlawful for you. To you He can make known His secrets, and to you He looks for an instant response to every requirement of His love. Your love and devotedness are His precious reward for all He has done for you. Do not let there be neither a day nor an hour in which you are not intelligently doing His will and following Him wholly. This personal service to Him will give a halo to your life.

GOD LOVES YOU

Hannah Whitall Smith

"Look at the birds of the air;
they do not sow or reap or store away in barns,
and yet your heavenly Father feeds them.
Are you not much more valuable than they?"
Matthew 6:26 NIV

When I read in the Bible that God is love, I am to believe it just because it is written and not because I have had any inward revelation that it is true. The Bible says that He cares for us as He cares for the lilies of the field and the birds of the air. The Bible says that the very hairs of our head are all numbered. I am to believe these statements just because they are written, no matter whether I have any inward revelation of it or not.

True humility accepts the love that is bestowed upon it and the gifts of that love with a meek and happy thankfulness, while pride shrinks from accepting gifts and is afraid to believe in the goodness of the one who gives them. Were we truly humble, we would accept God's love with thankful meekness.

It will sometimes look to us impossible that the Lord can love such disagreeable, unworthy beings as we feel ourselves to be. We must ignore these insinuations against the love of God as we would any insinuations against the love of our dearest friend. The fight to do this may sometimes be very severe. We must at once assert in definite words in our own hearts, and if possible aloud to someone, that God does love us. Our steadfast faith will unfailingly bring us, sooner or later, a glorious victory.

YIELD TO LOVE

JOHN CALVIN

Surely it was for my benefit that I suffered such anguish.
In your love you kept me from the pit of destruction;
you have put all my sins behind your back.
ISAIAH 38:17 NIV

Since the ungodly do not know that they are governed by
God's hand, they think that most of their troubles happen
by chance. The ungodly are like a wrongheaded young man,
who leaves his father's house and wanders far away. When
he all but perishes from hunger, cold, and other evils, he admits that he has met the just punishment of his stupidity. He
does not understand that his troubles are the chastisement
of his father. So the ungodly, having alienated themselves
from God and His household, do not understand that they
are still within the reach of God's hand.

Let us keep in mind that we cannot taste the love of
God in our afflictions unless we are persuaded that they are
rods with which our Father chastises us for our sins. Although God's hand falls upon those in His house and those
outside, it falls upon the former to show His special care for
them. The true solution of our problem is as follows: Anyone
who knows and is persuaded that God reprimands him must
promptly go on to consider that God afflicts him because
He loves him. For if God did not love him He would not
care about his salvation. God offers Himself as a Father to
all those who endure correction. In short then, when God
corrects us, He does so only as our Father, provided we yield
and obey.

LOVE THAT ACQUITS

CHARLES HADDON SPURGEON

Pursue righteousness and a godly life, along with faith, love, perseverance, and gentleness.
1 TIMOTHY 6:11 NLT

Jesus Christ came into the world to save sinners. I know that it is to me even to this day the greatest wonder that I ever heard of, that God should ever justify me. I feel myself to be a lump of unworthiness and a heap of sin apart from His almighty love. I know by a full assurance that I am justified by faith that is in Christ Jesus. Yet, by nature I must take my place among the most sinful. I am loved with as much love as if I had always been godly, although earlier I was ungodly. Who can help being astonished at this? Gratitude for such favor stands dressed in robes of wonder.

Have you lived without any love to God in your heart or regard to His commands in your life? You are the kind of person to whom this Gospel is sent—this Gospel which says that God justifies the ungodly. It is very wonderful, but it is available for you. It just suits you.

The salvation of God is for those who do not deserve it. The Lord only does that which is needful. Infinite wisdom never attempts that which is unnecessary. Jesus never undertakes that which is superfluous. To make him just who is just is no work for God. But to make him just who is unjust—that is work for infinite love and mercy. To justify the ungodly—this is a miracle worthy of God.

MOTHER'S LOVE

Hannah Whitall Smith

*"How often I have longed to gather your children together,
as a hen gathers her chicks under her wings."*
Matthew 23:37 niv

What a mother does for her foolish, careless, ignorant, but dearly loved little ones, this very thing our God does for us. When a mother is with her children, she thinks of their comfort and well-being always before her own. They must have comfortable seats where no cold air can reach them, no matter what amount of discomfort she may be compelled to endure. Their beds must be soft and their blankets warm; let hers be what they may. Their paths must be smooth and safe, although she is obliged to walk in rough and dangerous ways. Her own comfort, as compared with that of her children, is of no account in a loving mother's eyes. Surely our God has not made the mothers in this world more capable of a self-sacrificing love than He is Himself. He must be better and greater in love and self-sacrifice than any mother He ever made.

We may be perfectly sure that in even these little details of our lives we get the very best that His love, wisdom, and power can give us. He is so much better than any mother can be. His love is a wise love that sees the outcome of things and cares for our highest good. While a mother's weak love cannot see beyond the child's present comfort and cannot bear to inflict or allow any discomfort, the strong, wise love of our God can permit the present discomfort for the sake of the future glory that is to result.

GRACIOUS LOVE

Horatius Bonar

The Lord is compassionate and gracious,
slow to anger, abounding in love.
PSALM 103:8 NIV

Had God told us that He was not gracious, that He took no interest in our welfare, and that He had no intention of pardoning us, we could have no peace and no hope. In that case, our knowing God would only make us miserable. For how fearful a thing must it be to have the great God who made us, the great Father of Spirits, against us and not for us!

Strange to say, this is the very state of anxiety in which we may find many who profess to believe in God! With the Bible in their hands and the cross before their eyes, they wander on in a state of darkness and fear, such as would have arisen had God revealed Himself in hatred, not in love. They seem to believe the very opposite of what the Bible teaches us concerning God. They seem to attach a meaning to the cross that is the very opposite of what the Gospel declares. Had God been all frowns and the Bible all terrors and Christ all sternness, these people could not have been in a more troubled and uncertain state than that in which they are. How is this? Have they misunderstood the Bible? Have they mistaken the character of God, looking on Him as an austere man and a hard master?

But God has declared Himself gracious. God is love. The more, then, that we know of this God and of His grace, the more will His peace fill us.

AN INDIVIDUAL SAVIOR

CHARLES FINNEY

For their sake he remembered his covenant,
and showed compassion
according to the abundance of his steadfast love.
PSALM 106:45 NRSV

Toward whom is this love of God exercised? Toward us—
toward all beings of our lost race. To each one of us He
manifests this love.

How does He commend this love? By giving His Son
to die for us. By giving one who was a Son and a Son well-
beloved. It is written that God "gave Him a ransom for all"
and that "He tasted death for every man." We are not to
suppose that He died for the sum total of mankind in such
a sense that His death is not truly for each one in particular.
It is a great mistake into which some fall, to suppose that
Christ died for the human race in general and not for each
one in particular. By this mistake the Gospel is likely to lose
much of its practical power on our hearts. So we are to regard Jesus as having loved us personally and individually.

He would also commend the great strength of this love.
We should think we gave evidence of a strong love if we
were to give our friend a great sum of money. But what is
any sum of money compared with giving up a dear Son to
die? Oh, surely it is surpassing love, beyond measure wonderful, that Jesus should not only labor and suffer but should
really die! Was ever love like this?

COMFORTING LOVE

Hannah Whitall Smith

Finally, brethren, farewell. Become complete.
Be of good comfort, be of one mind, live in peace;
and the God of love and peace will be with you.
2 Corinthians 13:11 NKJV

God sent His Son to be the comforter of a mourning world. All through His life, the Lord Jesus Christ fulfilled His divine mission. For this is the glory of a religion of love. When His disciples asked Him to call down fire from heaven to consume some people who refused to receive Him, He turned and rebuked them. He came to save sinners. He had no other mission.

Two little girls were talking about God, and one said, "I know God does not love me. He could not care for such a teeny, tiny little girl as I am."

"Dear me, sis," said the other little girl, "don't you know that is just what God is for—to take care of teeny, tiny little girls who can't take care of themselves, just like us?"

"Is He?" said the first little girl. "I did not know that. Then I don't need to worry anymore, do I?"

If any troubled, doubting heart should read these lines, then let me tell you again in trumpet tones that this is just what the Lord Jesus Christ is for—to care for and comfort all who mourn. All who mourn, all who are cast down—I love to think of such a mission of comfort in a world of mourning like ours; and I long to see every cast down and sorrowing heart comforted with this comforting of God.

KNOW THE LOVE OF CHRIST

JOHN BUNYAN

I led them with cords of human kindness,
with bands of love.
I was to them like those who lift infants to their cheeks.
I bent down to them and fed them.
HOSEA 11:4 NRSV

We see the love of Christ in that the human nature, the nature of man, is taken into union with God. By this very act of the heavenly wisdom, we have an inconceivable pledge of the love of Christ to man. He took into union with Himself our nature. What did it signify but that He intended to take into union with Himself our person. For this very purpose, He assumed our nature. In that flesh He died for us, the just for the unjust, that He might bring us to God.

We may yet see more of His love in that He is gone into heaven, there to make ready and to prepare for us our mansions as if we were the lords and He the servant! This is love!

Also, we may see another degree of His love. Now in His absence, He has sent the third Person in the Trinity to supply in His place another comforter of us, that we may not think He forgot us. Yes, He has sent the Holy Spirit to fortify our spirits, and to strengthen us under all adversity.

He is now and has been ever since His ascension into glory laying out Himself as high priest for us. We also see yet more of His love by the fact that He will have us where He is, that we may see and be partakers of His glory.

LOVE THAT UNDERSTANDS

Hannah Whitall Smith

*O Lord, you have examined my heart
and know everything about me.*
Psalm 139:1 nlt

There are times when severe fever makes us utterly unaware of the presence of our most careful and tender nurses. A child in delirium will cry out in anguish for its mother. The child is being attended with the untold tenderness of a mother's love. Disease has hidden the mother from the child, but it has not hidden the child from the mother. In the same way, it is with our God and us. The darkness of our fears, sorrows, or despairs cannot hide us from God, although it often hides Him from us.

If we think of Him as a stern tyrant, intent only on His own glory, we shall be afraid of His continual presence. If we think of Him as a tender, loving Father, intent only on our blessing and happiness, we shall be glad and thankful to have Him with us. For the presence and the care of love can never mean anything but good to the one being loved.

Our God knows us and understands us, and is acquainted with all our ways. No one else in all the world understands us. Others misinterpret our actions and misjudge our motives. No one makes allowances for our ill health. No one realizes how much we have to contend with. But our heavenly Father knows it all. He understands us, and His judgment of us takes into account every element, conscious or unconscious, that goes to make up our character and to control our actions. Only an all-comprehending love can be just, and our God is just.

Turning Lackluster Religion into Spectacular Faith:

Overcoming Complacency

TRUE SATISFACTION

Hannah Whitall Smith

He who descended is the very one who ascended higher than all the heavens, in order to fill the whole universe. So Christ himself gave the apostles, the prophets, the evangelists, the pastors and teachers, to equip his people for works of service, so that the body of Christ may be built up until we all reach unity in the faith and in the knowledge of the Son of God and become mature, attaining to the whole measure of the fullness of Christ.
Ephesians 4:10–13 niv

No thoughtful person can question the fact that, for the most part, the Christian life, as it is generally lived, is not entirely a happy life. . . . You have carefully studied the holy scriptures and have gathered much precious truth from them, which you hoped would feed and nourish your spiritual life. But in spite of it all, your souls are starving and dying within you, and you cry out in secret, again and again, for that bread and water of life that you see promised in the scriptures to all believers.

Your early visions of triumph have seemed to grow dimmer and dimmer, and you have been forced to settle down to the conviction that the best you can expect from your religion is a life of alternate failure and victory, one hour sinning and the next repenting, and then beginning again, only to fail again, and again to repent.

But *is* this all? Had the Lord Jesus only this in His mind when He laid down His precious life to deliver you from your difficult and cruel bondage to sin? Was there a hidden reserve in each promise that was meant to deprive it of its complete fulfillment? Can we dream that the Savior, who was wounded for our transgressions and bruised for our iniquities, could possibly see of the travail of His soul and be satisfied in such Christian lives as fill the Church today? The Bible tells us that "for this purpose the Son of God was manifested, that he might destroy the works of the devil"; and can we imagine for a moment that this is beyond His power and that He finds Himself unable to accomplish the thing He came to earth to do?

In the very beginning, then, settle down on this one thing, that Jesus came to save you, now, in this life, from the power and dominion of sin and to make you more than conquerors through His power. If you doubt this, search your Bible and collect together every announcement or declaration concerning the purposes and object of His death on the cross. His work is to deliver us from our sins, from our bondage, from our defilement; and not a hint is given anywhere that this deliverance was limited and partial, one with which Christians so continually try to be satisfied.

LOVE IN HIS PRESENCE

RICHARD BAXTER

And they said one to another,
Did not our heart burn within us,
while he talked with us by the way,
and while he opened to us the scriptures?
LUKE 24:32 KJV

Now the poor soul complains, "I wish that I could love Christ more!" Then you cannot but love Him. Now, you know little of His agreeableness and therefore love little; then, your eyes will affect your heart, and the continual viewing of that perfect beauty will keep you in continual joy of love.

Christians, does it not now stir up your love to remember all the experiences of His love? Does not kindness melt you and the sunshine of divine goodness warm your frozen hearts? What will it do then, when you shall live in love, and have all in Him who is all? Christians, you will be then brimful of love; yet, love as much as you can, you shall be ten thousand times more beloved.

Were not the arms of the Son of God open upon the cross and an open passage made to His heart by the spear? Will not His arms and heart be open to you in glory? Did not He begin to love before you loved and will not He continue now? Did He love you an enemy, you a sinner, you who even loathed yourself? Did He accept you when you did disclaim yourself? And will He not now immeasurably love you as a son, as a perfect saint? He that in love wept over the old Jerusalem when near its ruin, with what love will He rejoice over the new Jerusalem in her glory!

LED BY LOVE

George Fox

Keep yourselves in the love of God;
look forward to the mercy of our Lord Jesus Christ
that leads to eternal life.
Jude 21 NRSV

Consider the everlasting love of God to my soul when I was in great distress! When my troubles were great, then was His love exceedingly great. All honor and glory be to You, Lord of Glory!

The Lord gently led me along and let me see His love, which was endless and eternal, surpassing all the knowledge that men have in the natural state or can obtain from history or books. His love let me see myself as I was—without Him.

I found that there were two thirsts in me—the one after the creature comforts and the other after the Lord, the Creator, and His Son Jesus Christ. I saw that all the world could do me no good. If I had had a king's diet, palace, and attendance, all would have been as nothing because nothing gave me comfort but the Lord by His power. I saw the great love of God and was filled with admiration at the infiniteness of it.

One day, when I had been walking alone and came home, I was taken up in the love of God. I could not but admire the greatness of His love. While I was in that condition, I clearly saw that all these troubles were good for me for the trial of my faith. I saw all through these troubles and temptations that my living faith was raised.

ABUSE OF LOVE

JOHN BUNYAN

I am shocked that you are turning away so soon from God,
who called you to himself through the loving mercy of Christ.
GALATIANS 1:6 NLT

Take heed of abusing the love of God. This exhortation seems needless because love is such a thing that one would think none could find in their heart to abuse. But I am of opinion that nothing is more abused among believers this day than the love of God. Lately, more light about the love of Christ broke out than formerly. Every child now can talk of the love of Christ. But this love of Christ has not been rightly applied by preachers or else not rightly received by believers. For never was this grace of Christ so turned into immorality as now.

But I say, let not this love of God and of Christ be abused. It is unnatural to abuse love. To abuse love is a villainy condemned of all. Yes, to abuse love is the most inexcusable sin of all. It is the sin of devils to abuse the love of God and of Christ. And what can one say for himself in the judgment who is charged with the abuse of love? Christians, deny yourselves, your lusts, and the vanities of this present life. Renounce the hidden things of dishonesty, walk not in craftiness, nor handle God's Word deceitfully. Devote yourselves to God. Become lovers of God and lovers of His ways. Then shall you show to all people that you have not received the grace of God in vain.

PERSONAL RESPONSIBILITY

CHARLES FINNEY

*For the Son of man is come to seek
and to save that which was lost.*
LUKE 19:10 KJV

I have often thought that the reason why so many pray only in form and not in heart for the salvation of souls is that they lack love like God's love for the souls of the perishing. They lack a sense of personal responsibility for the lost.

You must see impressively that souls are precious. Without such a sense of the value of souls, you will not pray with fervent, strong desire. Without a just apprehension of their guilt, danger, and remedy, you will not pray in faith for God's interposing grace.

Indeed, you must have so much of the love of God—a love like God's love for sinners—in your soul that you are ready for any sacrifice or any labor. You need to feel as God feels. He so loved the world that He gave His only begotten Son, that whosoever should believe in Him might not perish.

You need so to love the world that your love will draw you to make similar sacrifices and put forth similar labors. Love for souls, the same in kind as God had in giving up His Son to die and as Christ had in coming cheerfully down to make Himself the offering, each servant of God must have. Otherwise, your prayers will have little heart and no power with God. This love for souls is always implied in acceptable prayer, that God would send forth laborers into His harvest.

TENDER LOVE

Hannah Whitall Smith

"For the Lord disciplines those whom he loves,
and chastises every child whom he accepts."
Hebrews 12:6 NRSV

Sometimes everything seems so firmly established in prosperity that no dream of disaster disturbs us. Our reputation is assured, our efforts have all been successful beyond our hopes, and our soul is at ease. The need for God is in danger of becoming far-off and vague. Then the Lord is obliged to put an end to it all, and our prosperity crumbles around us like a house built on sand.

We are tempted to think He is angry with us. But in truth, it is not anger but tender love. His very love compels Him to take away the outward prosperity that is keeping our souls from entering the interior spiritual kingdom for which we long. When the fig tree ceases to blossom and there is no fruit in the vines, when the flock shall be cut off from the fold and there shall be no herd in the stalls, then, and often not until then, will our souls learn to rejoice in the Lord only and to joy in the God of our salvation.

It might look as far as the outward seeing goes as though it were God's wrath that did this. Many a frightened Christian thinks it is. But His wrath is not against us. His love could do no less than destroy these refuges in order that we may be delivered. Paul declared that he counted all things but loss that he might win Christ. When we learn to say the same, the peace and joy that the Gospel promises become our permanent possession.

BRAVE LOVE

Thomas à Kempis

But let us, who are of the day, be sober,
putting on the breastplate of faith and love;
and for an helmet, the hope of salvation.
1 Thessalonians 5:8 kjv

The brave lover stands firm in temptations and pays no heed to the crafty persuasions of the enemy. As Jesus pleases him in prosperity, so in adversity Jesus is not displeasing to him. The wise lover regards not so much the gift of Him who loves as the love of Him who gives. He regards the affection of the Giver rather than the value of the gift and sets his Beloved above all gifts. The noble lover does not rest in the gift but in Jesus who is above every gift.

All is not lost, then, if you sometimes feel less devout than you wish toward Jesus. That good and sweet feeling which you sometimes have is the effect of present grace and a certain foretaste of your heavenly home. It is not an illusion that you are sometimes engrossed in intense joy and then quickly returned to the usual follies of your heart. For these are evils that you suffer rather than commit. So long as they displease you and you struggle against them, it is a matter of merit and not a loss.

You must know that the old enemy tries by all means in his power to hinder your desire for good and to turn you from every devotional practice. He suggests many evil thoughts that he may cause you weariness and horror and draw you away from prayer and holy reading.

Fight like a good soldier, and if you sometimes fall through weakness, rise again with greater strength than before, trusting in Christ's most abundant grace.

TO LIVE IS TO LOVE

Henry Drummond

*And the grace of our Lord was exceeding abundant
with faith and love which is in Christ Jesus.*
1 Timothy 1:14 KJV

Let the first great object of our lives be to achieve the character that is built around love. Never offer people a thimbleful of Gospel. Do not offer them merely joy, merely peace, merely rest, or merely safety. Tell them how Christ came to give men a more abundant life than they have, a life abundant in love. Many of the current religious teachings are addressed only to a part of a person's nature. They offer peace, not life; faith, not love; justification, not regeneration. And people slip back again from such religion because it has never really held them.

To love abundantly is to live abundantly, and to love forever is to live forever. Therefore, eternal life is inextricably bound up with love. We want to live forever for the same reason that we want to live tomorrow. Why do you want to live tomorrow? It is because there is someone who loves you, and whom you want to see tomorrow, be with, and love back. There is no other reason why we should live on than that we love and are beloved. No worse fate can befall a man in this world than to live and grow old alone, unloving, and unloved. So long as he has friends—those who love him and whom he loves—he will live, because to live is to love. Love must be eternal. It is what God is. Love is life. Love never fails, and life never fails so long as there is love.

LOVE AND SPIRITUAL SICKNESS

THOMAS WATSON

O taste and see that the Lord is good;
happy are those who take refuge in him.
PSALM 34:8 NRSV

Sometimes when people are sick, they lose interest in eating. They do not find a savory relish in their food. When Christians find no sweetness in God's promises, it is a sign of a spiritual sickness. At one time they did find comfort in drawing near to God. His Word was as honey, very delicious to their soul, but now it is otherwise. They can taste no more sweetness in spiritual things than in the white of an egg. To lose the taste indicates the loss of the first love. They have no appetite, they do not so prize Christ, and they have no strong affections to the Word. Sadly, their love is decaying.

When Christians grow more in love with the world, it indicates a decrease of spiritual love. Their thoughts and interests are still bound to the earth. It is a sign they are going downhill quickly and their love for God is declining. When rust attacks a metal, it takes away the brightness and corrodes the metal. In the same way, when the world clings to people's souls, it not only hinders the shining luster of their graces, but by degrees it corrodes them.

Love is a grace that Christians do not know how to be without. A soldier may as well be without his weapons, an artist without his pencil, a musician without his instrument as a Christian without love. How careful then should we be to keep alive our love for God!

THE LUSTER OF LOVE

Thomas Watson

Love the Lord, all you his saints.
The Lord preserves the faithful,
but abundantly repays the one who acts haughtily.
Psalm 31:23 NRSV

There are but few who love God. Many give Him hypocriti-
cal kisses, but few love Him. The wicked would flee from
God; they would neither be under His rules nor within His
reach. They fear God but do not love Him. All the strength
in men or angels cannot make the heart love God.

Without love, all our religion is vain. It is not how much
we do but how much we love. If a servant does not do his
work willingly and out of love, it is not acceptable. Duties
not mingled with love are as burdensome to God as they
are to us. David therefore counsels his son Solomon to serve
God with a willing mind. To do duty without love is not
sacrifice but penance.

Love is a pure flame kindled from heaven. By it we re-
semble God, who is love. Believing and obeying do not make
us to be like God, but by love we grow to be like Him. Love is
a grace which most delights in God and is most delightful to
Him. Love puts a flourishing and luster upon all the graces.
The graces seem to be eclipsed, unless love shines and sparkles
in them. Faith is not true unless it works by love. The waters
of repentance are not pure unless they flow from the spring of
love. Love is the incense that makes all our services fragrant
and acceptable to God.

LOVE DOES NOT GROW TIRED

Thomas à Kempis

*For I desire steadfast love and not sacrifice,
the knowledge of God rather than burnt offerings.*
Hosea 6:6 NRSV

One who is in love flies, runs, and rejoices. He is free, not bound. He gives all for all and has all in all. Love often knows no limits but overflows all bounds. Love feels no burden, thinks nothing of troubles, attempts more than it is able, and does not plead impossibility because it believes that it may and can do all things. For this reason the one with love is able to do all, performing and effecting much, but he who does not love falls and fails.

Love is watchful. Sleeping, it does not slumber. Wearied, it is not tired. Pressed, it is not restricted. Alarmed, it is not confused. Love is swift, sincere, kind, pleasant, and delightful. Love is strong, patient and faithful, prudent, and long-suffering. Love is never self-seeking because in whatever a person seeks for himself, there he falls from love. Love is circumspect, humble, and upright. It is not intent upon vain things. It is sober and chaste, firm and quiet, guarded in all the senses.

He who is not ready to suffer all things and to stand resigned to the will of the Beloved is not worthy to be called a lover. A lover must embrace willingly all that is difficult and bitter for the sake of the Beloved, and he should not turn away from Him because of adversities.

LOVE FOR THE CHURCH

CHARLES HADDON SPURGEON

No one hates his own body but feeds and cares for it,
just as Christ cares for the church.
EPHESIANS 5:29 NLT

God loves the church with a love too deep for human imagination. He loves her with all His infinite heart. Therefore let the church be of good courage. The Lord says, "I am jealous for Jerusalem and for Zion with a great jealousy." The Lord loves His church so much that He cannot bear that she should go astray to others. When she has done so, He cannot endure that she should suffer too much or too heavily. He will not have His enemies afflict her. He is displeased with them because they increase her misery. When God seems most to leave His church, His heart is warm toward her.

History shows that whenever God uses a rod to chasten His servants, He always breaks it afterward as if He loathed the rod that gave His children pain. Like as a father pities his children, so the Lord pities them who fear Him.

If this is true of His church collectively, it is also true of each individual member. You may fear that the Lord has passed you by, but it is not so. He who counts the stars and calls them by their names is in no danger of forgetting His own children. He knows your case as thoroughly as if you were the only creature He ever made or the only saint He ever loved. Approach Him, and be at peace.

LOVE IN THE HEART

Jonathan Edwards

*"For the LORD does not see as man sees;
for man looks at the outward appearance,
but the LORD looks at the heart."*
1 SAMUEL 16:7 NKJV

Ask yourself whether you have ever in your life brought forth any fruit to God. Have you ever done anything from a gracious respect to God or out of love to God? By only seeking your worldly interest, you do not bring forth fruit to God. To be sober, moral, and religious only to be seen of men or out of respect to your own credit and honor does not bring forth fruit to God. How is doing that for God, which is only for the sake of custom or to be esteemed of men?

For men to pray, read, hear, and to be strict and diligent in religious and moral duties merely from the fear of hell does not bring fruit to God. What thanks are due to you for being willing to take some pains to escape burning in hell for all eternity? There is never a devil in hell but would gladly do the same.

There is no fruit brought forth to God where there is nothing done from love to God or from any true respect to Him. God looks at the heart. He does not stand in need of our services, neither is He benefited by anything that we can do. He does not receive anything of us because it benefits Him but only as a suitable testimony of our love and respect to Him. This is the fruit that He seeks.

JOY AND HAPPINESS

ANDREW MURRAY

Satisfy us in the morning with your unfailing love,
that we may sing for joy and be glad all our days.
PSALM 90:14 NIV

If anyone asks the question, "How can I be a happy Christian?" our Lord's answer is very simple: "I have spoken to you, that My joy may be in you, and that your joy may be fulfilled." To many Christians the thought of a life wholly dwelling in Christ is one of strain and painful effort. They cannot see that the strain and effort only come when we do not yield ourselves unreservedly to the life of Christ in us.

We are to have Christ's own joy in us. And what is Christ's own joy? There is no joy like love. There is no joy but love. Christ had spoken of the Father's love and His own residing in joy, and of His having loved us with that same love. His joy is nothing but the joy of love, of being loved and of loving. He wants us to share the joy of being loved of the Father by our loving and living for those around us. This is just the joy of being truly branches—living in His love and then giving up ourselves in love to bear fruit for others.

Religion is meant to be in everyday life a thing of unspeakable joy. And why do so many complain that it is not so? They do so because they do not believe there is joy like the joy of living in Christ and in His love.

LOVE IN ACTION

THOMAS WATSON

Place me like a seal over your heart,
like a seal on your arm;
for love is as strong as death,
its jealousy unyielding as the grave.
It burns like blazing fire, like a mighty flame.
SONG OF SOLOMON 8:6 NIV

Love to God must be active. Love is no idle ornament. It sets the head studying for God and the feet running in the ways of His commandments. Pretenses of love are insufficient. Love has not only a smooth tongue but also a kind heart. He will be eyes to the blind and feet to the lame. The bellies of the poor shall be where he sows the golden seeds of liberality. Some say they love God, but their love is lame because they give nothing to good uses. Indeed, faith deals with invisibles, but God hates that love which is invisible. Love vents itself in good works.

He who is a lover of God gives Him such a love as he bestows upon none else. Love to God is permanent. Love is like the pulse of the body, always beating. It is not a desert but a spring flood. Nothing can hinder a Christian's love to God. Nothing can conquer love, not any difficulties or oppositions. Neither the sweet waters of pleasure nor the bitter waters of persecution can quench love. Love to God abides firm to death. Light things, such as chaff and feathers, are quickly blown away, but a tree that is rooted survives the storm. He who is rooted in love endures. True love never ends.

STEPPING-STONES OF LOVE

F. B. Meyer

"Indeed, he loves his people;
all his holy ones are in his hands.
They follow in his steps
and accept his teaching."
Deuteronomy 33:3 NLT

The facts in the Bible are like stepping-stones across a brook. Before you reach the shallows where they lie, you wonder how you will get over. But on stepping down to the edge of the water, you see that they span the space from bank to bank. You must come down to them, see how strongly fixed they are in the oozy bed, and notice how easily the villagers cross. Then you will be able to trust them. Finally, with a light heart and great sense of relief, you step from one to another.

It is a fact that God loves each of us with the most tender and most special love. You may not believe or feel it. The warm summer sun may be shining against your shuttered and curtained window without making itself seen or felt within. Your failure to realize and appreciate the fact of God's love toward you cannot alter it being so.

After the peace was signed between the North and the South in the great American Civil War, there were soldiers hiding in the woods and starving on berries, who might have returned to their homes. They either did not know or did not credit the Good News. They went on starving long after their comrades had been welcomed by their wives and children. Theirs was the loss, but their failure in knowledge or belief did not alter the fact that peace was proclaimed and that the door was wide open for their return.

HALFHEARTED LOVE

DWIGHT LYMAN MOODY

My goal is that they may be encouraged in heart
and united in love,
so that they may have the full riches of
complete understanding.
COLOSSIANS 2:2 NIV

I have learned that when anyone becomes in earnest about his soul's salvation, and he begins to seek God, it does not take long for an anxious sinner to meet an anxious Savior. Those who seek for Him with all their hearts, find Christ.

I am tired and sick of halfheartedness. I don't like a halfhearted man. I don't care for anyone to love me half-heartedly. And the Lord won't have it. If we are going to seek for Him and find Him, we must do it with all our hearts.

I believe the reason why so few find Christ is that they do not search for Him with all their hearts. Everything God has done proves that He is in earnest about the salvation of men's souls. And the Lord wants us to be in earnest when it comes to this great question of the soul's salvation. I never saw men seeking Him with all their hearts but they soon found Him.

It was quite refreshing one night to find a young man who thought he was not worth saving, he was so vile and wicked. There was hope for him because he was so desperately in earnest about his soul. He had a sight of himself in God's looking glass and had a very poor opinion of himself. But the moment he sees God by the eye of faith, he is down on his knees, and, like Job, he cries, "Behold, I am vile."

OBEDIENT LOVE

Elizabeth Prentiss

And without faith it is impossible to please God, because anyone
who comes to him must believe that he exists and that he rewards
those who earnestly seek him.
Hebrews 11:6 NIV

I went to [a faith] meeting and so did Amelia. A great many
young people were there and a few children. Dr. Cabot
[the pastor] went about from seat to seat, speaking to each
one separately. When he came to us, I expected he would
say something about the way in which I had been brought
up and reproach me for not profiting more by the instruc-
tions and example I had at home. Instead of that he said in
a cheerful voice, "Well, my dear, I cannot see into your heart
and positively tell whether there is love to God there or not.
But I suppose you have come today in order to let me help
you find out?"

I said, "Yes"; that was all I could get out.

"Let me see, then," he went on. "Do you love your
mother?"

I said, "Yes," once more.

"But prove to me that you do. How do you know it?"

I tried to think. Then I said, "I feel that I love her. I love to
love her; I like to be with her. I like to hear people praise her.
And I try—sometimes at least—to do things to please her.
But I don't try half as hard as I ought, and I do and say a great
many things to displease her. . ."

"In the first place, then, you feel that you love your mother?
But you never feel that you love your God and Savior?"

"I often try and try, but I never do," I said.

"Love won't be forced," he said quickly.

"Then what shall I do?"

"In the second place, you like to be with your mother.

But you never like to be with the Friend who loves you so much better than she does?"

"I don't know; I never was with Him. Sometimes I think that when Mary sat at His feet and heard Him talk, she must have been very happy."

"We come to the third test, then. You like to hear people praise your mother. And have you never rejoiced to hear the Lord magnified?"

I shook my head sorrowfully enough.

"Let us then try the last test. You know you love your mother because you try to do things to please her. That is, to do what you know she wishes you to do? Very well. Have you never tried to do anything God wishes you to do?"

"Oh yes; often. But not so often as I ought."

"Of course not. No one does that. But come now, why do you try to do what you think will please Him? Because it is easy? Because you like to do what He likes rather than what you like yourself?"

I tried to think and got puzzled.

"Never mind," said Dr. Cabot. "I have come now to the point I was aiming at. You cannot prove to yourself that you love God by examining your feelings toward Him. They are indefinite and they fluctuate. But just as far as you obey Him, just so far, depend upon it, you love Him. It is not natural to us sinful, ungrateful human beings to prefer His pleasure to our own or to follow His way instead of our own way, and nothing, nothing but love of Him can or does make us obedient to Him."

"Couldn't we obey Him from fear?" Amelia now asked. She had been listening all this time in silence.

"Yes; and so you might obey your mother from fear but only for a season. If you had no real love for her, you would gradually cease to dread her displeasure; whereas it is in the very nature of love to grow stronger and more influential every hour."

"You mean, then, that if we want to know whether we

love God, we must find out whether we are obeying Him?" Amelia asked.

"I mean exactly that. 'He that hath my commandments, and keepeth them, he it is that loveth me'" (John 14:21 KJV).

. . . .When we got out into the street, Amelia and I got hold of each other's hands. We did not speak a word till we reached the door, but we knew that we were as good friends as ever.

"I understand all Dr. Cabot said," Amelia whispered as we separated. But I felt like one in a fog. I cannot see how it is possible to love God and yet feel as stupid as I do when I think of Him. Still, I am determined to do one thing, and that is to pray regularly instead of now and then, as I have got in the habit of doing lately.

GROUNDED IN LOVE

JOHN BUNYAN

Not to us, O Lord, not to us,
but to your name give glory,
for the sake of your steadfast love
and your faithfulness.
PSALM 115:1 NRSV

Why should anything have my heart but Christ? He loves me; He loves me with love that goes beyond knowledge. He loves me, and He shall have me. He loves me, and I will love Him. His love stripped Him of all for my sake. Lord, let my love strip me of all for Your sake. I am a son of love, an object of love, a monument of love, of love freely given, of distinguishing love, of special love, and of love that passes knowledge. I walk in love—in love to God, in love to men, in holy love, and in genuine love.

Let the upright speak of love that is taken with love, that is captivated with love, that is carried away with love. If the upright speaks of love, his speaking signifies something. The powers and bands of love are upon him, and he shows to all that he knows what he is speaking of. But the very mentioning of love in the mouth of the profane is like a parable in the mouth of fools or as salt unsavory.

If you would improve this love, keep yourself in it. He who would live a sweet, comfortable, joyful life must live a very holy life. To this end, you must take root and be grounded in love; that is, you must be well settled and established in this love, if indeed you would improve it.

IMAGE OF CHRIST

CHARLES FINNEY

If you have any encouragement from being united with Christ,
if any comfort from his love, if any common sharing in the Spirit,
if any tenderness and compassion, then make my joy complete
by being like-minded, having the same love,
being one in spirit and of one mind.
PHILIPPIANS 2:1–2 NIV

When Christians have sunk down into a low state, they neither have nor can have the same love and confidence toward each other as when they are all alive and active and living holy lives. If Christian love is the love of the image of Christ in His people, then it can be exercised only where that image really exists. Merely knowing that they belong to the church, or seeing them occasionally at the communion table, will not produce Christian love unless they see the image of Christ.

Nothing but a revival can restore Christian love and confidence among church members. There is no other way to wake up that love of Christians for one another which is sometimes felt when they have such love as they cannot express. You cannot have such love without confidence, and you cannot restore confidence without such evidence of piety as is seen in a revival.

So if a member of the church finds his brethren cold toward him, there is but one way to restore it. It is by being revived himself and pouring out from his eyes and from his life the splendor of the image of Christ. This spirit will catch and spread in the church, confidence will be renewed, and brotherly love will prevail again.

LOVE THE LAW

THOMAS WATSON

Oh, how I love your law!
I meditate on it all day long.
PSALM 119:97 NIV

If we are lovers of God, we love what God loves. We love
God's Word. David esteemed the Word for the sweetness
of it above honey and for the value of it above gold. The lines
of scripture are richer than the mines of gold. Well may we
love the Word—it is a guiding star that directs us to heaven.
That man who does not love the Word but thinks it too
strict and could wish any part of the Bible torn out, has not
the least spark of love in his heart.

A gracious soul loves God's laws and is glad of the law
because it checks his sinful excesses. The heart would be
ready to run wild in sin if it had not some blessed restraints
put upon it by the law of God. He who loves God loves His
law—the law of repentance, the law of self-denial.

Many say they love God, but they hate His laws. God's
precepts are compared to cords: they bind men to their good
behavior, but the wicked think these cords too tight; therefore, they say, "Let us break them." They pretend to love
Christ as a Savior but hate Him as a king. Sinners would
have Christ put a crown upon their head but not a yoke
upon their neck. He would be a strange king who should
rule without laws.

MOLDED IN LOVE

ANDREW MURRAY

But we know that when Christ appears,
we shall be like him,
for we shall see him as he is.
1 JOHN 3:2 NIV

The first and chief need of our Christian life is fellowship with God. As I need every moment fresh air to breathe, as the sun every moment sends down its light, so it is only in direct living communication with God that my soul can be strong. Let God's love overwhelm you and bow you still lower down. Sink down before Him in humility, meekness, patience, and surrender to His goodness and mercy. Then accept and value your place in Christ Jesus. He loves you with a personal love. He looks every day for the personal response of your love. Look into His face with trust until His love really shines into your heart. Make His heart glad by telling Him that you do love Him. He offers Himself to you as a personal Savior and Keeper from the power of sin.

We have not only Christ's life in us as a power, and His presence with us as a person, but we have His likeness to be clearly apparent in us. He is to be formed in us so that His form and His likeness can be seen in us. The God who revealed Jesus in the flesh and perfected Him will reveal Him in you and perfect you in Him. The Father loves the Son and delights to work out His image and likeness in you. Count upon it that this blessed work will be done in you as you wait on your God and hold fellowship with Him.

UNDERTRUSTED LOVE

Hannah Whitall Smith

But I trusted in your steadfast love;
my heart shall rejoice in your salvation.
Psalm 13:5 nrsv

I was once talking to an intelligent agnostic. He said, "The Christians I meet seem to me to be the very most uncomfortable people anywhere around. They seem to carry their religion as a man carries a headache. He does not want to get rid of his head, but at the same time, it is very uncomfortable to have it."

This was a lesson I have never forgotten. It seemed, as one of my Christian friends said to me one day when we were comparing our experiences, "as if we had just enough religion to make us miserable."

I confess that being uncomfortable with religion was very disappointing. I had expected something altogether different. It seemed to me exceedingly odd that a religion whose fruits were declared in the Bible to be love, joy, and peace should so often work out practically in an exactly opposite direction and should develop the fruits of doubt, fear, unrest, conflict, and discomforts of every kind. Why should the children of God lead such utterly uncomfortable religious lives when He has led us to believe that His yoke would be easy and His burden light? Why do we find it so hard to be sure that God really loves us?

The religion of the Lord Jesus Christ was meant to be full of comfort, because "eye hath not seen, nor ear heard, neither have entered into the heart of man, the things which God hath prepared for them that love him" (1 Corinthians 2:9 kjv). All the difficulty arises from the fact that we have underbelieved and undertrusted.

KEEP LOVE BURNING

THOMAS WATSON

*"And because of the increase of lawlessness,
the love of many will grow cold."*
MATTHEW 24:12 NRSV

You who have love to God, labor to preserve it. As you would have God's love to be continued to you, let your love be continued to Him. Love, as fire, will be ready to go out. Satan labors to blow out this flame, and through neglect of duty we lose it. A baby's tender body without clothes is likely to get cold. So when we leave off duty, we cool in our love to God. Of all graces, love is most apt to fade; therefore, we need to be the more careful to preserve it. It is sad to see believers declining in their love to God.

When duties of religion are performed in a dead, formal matter, this is a sad symptom of decay in our first love. If the strings of a violin are slack, the violin can never make good music. Believers who grow slack in duty can never make any harmonious sound in God's ears. When spiritual action is slow and the pulse of the soul beats low, it is a sign that Christians have left their first love.

Watch your hearts every day. Take notice of the first declining in love. Observe yourselves when you begin to grow dull and listless, and use all means for quickening. Be much in prayer, meditation, and holy discussion. When the fire is going out, you throw on fuel. So when the flame of your love is going out, make use of Gospel principles and promises as fuel to keep the fire of your love burning.

Making It Personal:

What's Your Love Story?

THE LORD IS GOOD

Hannah Whitall Smith

Now that you have tasted that the Lord is good.
1 Peter 2:3 NIV

I shall never forget the hour when I first discovered that God was really good. It had never dawned on me that it meant He was actually and practically good, with the same kind of goodness He has commanded us to have. The expression "the goodness of God" had seemed to me nothing more than a sort of heavenly statement, which I could not be expected to understand. Then one day in my reading of the Bible I came across the words "O taste and see that the Lord is good" and suddenly they meant something. What does it mean to be good?

To be good is to do the best we know. I saw that since God has total knowledge He must know what is the best and highest good of all; therefore, His goodness must necessarily be beyond question.

I can never express what this meant to me. I had such a view of the actual goodness of God that I saw nothing could possibly go wrong under His care, and it seemed to me that no one could ever be anxious again. Over and over, when appearances have been against Him, and when I have been tempted to question whether He had been unkind or neglectful or indifferent, I have been brought up short by the words "the Lord is good." I have seen that it was simply unthinkable that a God who was good could have done the bad things I had imagined.

TALKING TO GOD

SOJOURNER TRUTH

Hold fast the form of sound words,
which thou hast heard of me,
in faith and love which is in Christ Jesus.
2 TIMOTHY 1:13 KJV

Sojourner Truth's mother talked to her of God. From these conversations, her mind drew the conclusion that God was a great man and, being located high in the sky, could see all that transpired on the earth. She believed He not only saw but also noted down all her actions in a great book.

At first, she heard Jesus mentioned in reading or speaking but had received from what she heard no impression that He was any other than an eminent man, like a Washington or a Lafayette. Now He appeared to her so mild, so good, and so every way lovely, and He loved her so much! And, how strange that He had always loved her and she had never known it! And how great a blessing He conferred, in that He should stand between her and God! And God was no longer a terror and a dread to her.

She stopped not to argue the point, even in her own mind, whether He had reconciled her to God or God to herself, being but too happy that God was no longer to her as a consuming fire and Jesus was altogether lovely. Her heart was now full of joy and gladness, as it had been of terror and at one time of despair. In the light of her great happiness, the world was clad in new beauty—the very air sparkled as with diamonds and was redolent of heaven.

STANDING ON THE PROMISES OF LOVE

F. B. MEYER

*Has not God chosen those who are poor
in the eyes of the world to be rich in faith
and to inherit the kingdom he promised
those who love him?*
JAMES 2:5 NIV

In earlier life I used to seek after greater faith by consider-ing how great God was, how rich and how strong. Why should He not give me money for His work, since He was so rich? Why not carry the entire burden of my responsibili-ties, since He was so mighty? These considerations helped me less, however, than my now certain conviction that He is absolutely faithful. He is faithful to His promises and faith-ful to the soul that at His clear call has stepped out into any enterprise for Him.

We may lose heart and hope, our head may turn dizzy, our heart faint, and the mocking voices of our foes suggest that God has forgotten or forsaken us. But He remains faith-ful. He cannot deny Himself. He cannot throw aside respon-sibilities that He has assumed. Often I have gone to God in desperate need, aggravated by nervous depression and heart sickness, and said, "My faith is flickering out. Its hand seems paralyzed, its eye blinded, its old glad song silenced forever. But You are faithful, and I am counting on You!"

The soul loves to stand upon the promises of God. We find no difficulty in trusting our friends because we open our hearts, like south windows, to their love. Where would be our difficulty about faith if we ceased worrying about it and were occupied with the object of faith—Jesus Christ our Lord?

HE LOVES PEOPLE

HENRY DRUMMOND

*"Because the LORD loves his people,
he has made you their king."*
2 CHRONICLES 2:11 NIV

You have heard of Helen Keller who was born deaf, unable to speak, and blind. Until she was seven years of age, her life was an absolute blank. Nothing could go into that mind because the ears and eyes were closed to the outer world. Then they began to put in little bits of knowledge and bit by bit to educate her.

But they reserved the religious instruction for Phillips Brooks. When she was twelve years old, they took her to him, and he talked to her through the young lady who had been the means of opening her senses and who could communicate with her by the exceedingly delicate process of touch. Phillips Brooks began to tell her about God and what He had done and how He loves people and what He is to us.

The child listened very intelligently and finally said, "Mr. Brooks, I knew all of that before, but I did not know His name." Have you not often felt something within you that was not you, some mysterious pressure, some impulse, some guidance, something lifting you and impelling you to do that which you would not yourself ever have conceived of? Perhaps you did not know His name—it is God who works in you. If we can really build our life upon that great, simple fact, the first principle of religion which we are so prone to forget—that God is with us and in us—we will have no difficulty or fear about our future life.

REBELLION AND LOVE

Reuben Archer Torrey

*They refused to obey, and were not mindful of the wonders
that you performed among them. . . But you are a God
ready to forgive. . .and abounding in steadfast love.*
Nehemiah 9:17 nrsv

A boy was sick a little time before, and the mother had
watched over him so faithfully and tenderly that she had
caught his sickness. She had brought him back to health, but
she was lying very sick. She had told the boy and his sister
that they could go out into the garden, and said, "There are
some flowers out there about which I am very careful. I do
not want you to pick them."

So Johnny and Mary go out, and Johnny goes to work to
do just what he was asked not to do. His sister says, "Johnny,
did you not hear Mother tell us not to pick those flowers?
Why pick them?"

"Because," says Johnny, "she loves me so, Mary. Don't
you know how she loves me; how when I was sick, Mother
gave up sleep and everything, and watched over me through
the nights? Don't you know that she is sick there now because she loves me so? And so I am now going to do the very
thing she told me not to do."

What would you think of a boy like that? And what do
you think of the man or woman who make their boast of the
love of God, and because God loves them, make God's love
an excuse for rebellion against Him, and make God's love a
reason for a worldly life?

LOVE AND THE CANNIBALS

JOHN G. PATON

"Because he loves me," says the LORD,
"I will rescue him;
I will protect him, for he acknowledges my name."
PSALM 91:14 NIV

One day while working as a missionary on the Pacific island of Tanna, I heard an unusual bleating among my few remaining goats, as if they were being killed. I rushed to the goat house and found myself instantly surrounded by a band of armed men. Their weapons were raised, and I expected the next moment to die. But God moved me to talk to them firmly and kindly. I warned them of their sin and its punishment. I showed them that only my love and pity led me to remain there seeking their good, and that if they killed me, they killed their best friend. I further assured them I was not afraid to die, for at death my Savior would take me to heaven and that I would be far happier than on earth. My only desire to live was to make them happy by teaching them to love Jesus Christ my Lord.

I then lifted up my hands and eyes to the heavens and prayed aloud for Jesus to bless all the Tannese and to protect me or take me to heaven as He saw to be for the best. One after another, they slipped away from me, and Jesus restrained them again. Did ever a mother run more quickly to protect her crying child in danger's hour than the Lord Jesus hastens to answer believing prayer and send help to His servants?

CHRISTLIKE LOVE

Hannah Whitall Smith

I pray that. . .
Christ may dwell in your hearts through faith.
Ephesians 3:16–17 niv

If Christ is dwelling in my heart, I must necessarily be Christlike. I cannot be unkind or irritable, self-seeking or dishonest. His gentleness, sweetness, tender compassion, and loving submission to the will of His Father must be manifested in my daily walk. The life of Jesus is to be made obvious in our lives. Are we so conformed to the image of Christ that people in seeing us see a glimpse of Him, also?

A minister's wife told me that at one time they had moved to a new place. Her little boy came in after the first afternoon of play. He exclaimed joyfully, "Mother, I have found such a lovely, good little girl to play with that I never want to go away again."

"I am very glad, darling," said the loving mother, delighted because of her child's happiness. "What is the little girl's name?"

The child replied with a sudden solemnity, "I think her name is Jesus."

"Frank!" exclaimed the mother. "What do you mean?"

He said deprecatingly, "She was so lovely that I did not know what she could be called but Jesus."

Are our lives so Christlike that anyone could have such a thought of us? Is it apparent to all around us that we have been with Jesus? Unfortunately, it is often just the contrary. Are some of us so cross and uncomfortable in our living that exactly the opposite thing would have to be said about us?

LOVE AND THE UNBELIEVING SON

EDWARD MCKENDREE BOUNDS

For you, O Lord, are good and forgiving,
abounding in steadfast love to all who call on you.
PSALM 86:5 NRSV

A mother asked a minister of the Gospel to visit her son to win him to Christ. The preacher found the young man's mind full of skeptical notions and impervious to argument. Finally the young man was asked to pray, just once, for light. He replied: "I do not know anything perfect to whom or to which I could pray."

"How about your mother's love?" said the preacher. "Isn't that perfect? Hasn't she always stood by you, been ready to take you in and care for you when even your father had really kicked you out?"

The young man choked with emotion and said, "Y–e–s, sir, that is so."

"Then pray to love—it will help you. Will you promise?"

He promised.

That night the young man prayed in the privacy of his room. He kneeled down, closed his eyes, and struggling a moment uttered the words: "O love." Instantly as by a flash of lightning, the Bible text came to him: "God is love." He said brokenly, "O God!" Then another flash of divine truth, and a voice said, "God so loved the world that He gave His only begotten Son." Then instantly he exclaimed, "O Christ, You are divine love; show me light and truth." It was all over. He was in the light of the most perfect peace. He ran downstairs and told his mother.

That young man is today an eloquent minister of Jesus Christ.

ASSURED LOVE

John Henry Jowett

To those who have been called,
who are loved in God the Father
and kept for Jesus Christ: Mercy, peace and love
be yours in abundance.
Jude 1–2 niv

When I recall a prominent Christian friend, I am conscious of the sweet and gracious perfume that was ever rising from his full and ever-moving life. At the heart of this busy worker was the restful lover. He moved about in assured and certain warfare because his soul was ever feasting in a companionship of love with his Lord. I like this sentence of his: "What a thrill it gives me to meet with one who has fallen in love with Jesus!" Yes, that is the speech of a lover who is himself in love with the Lord. It is the thrill of sympathetic vibrations. It is the thrill of one who is already in love with Jesus and who delights to see Jesus come to His own. This renowned Christian's sort of warfare finds its explanation in the lover's thrill, and in a lover's thrill, has its secret in the lover's tranquillity.

But why should I keep upon these high planes of renowned and prominent personalities? Get a person who is restfully intimate with his Lord and you have a person whose force is tremendous! Such people move in apparent ease, but it is the ease that is linked with the infinite; it is the very peace of God. They may be engaged in apparent trifles, but even in the doing of the trifles there emerges the health-giving currents of the kingdom of God.

HAVE CONFIDENCE

Hannah Whitall Smith

For no matter how many promises God has made,
they are "Yes" in Christ.
And so through him the "Amen" is spoken by us
to the glory of God.
2 Corinthians 1:20 NIV

Often it has happened to me to find, on awaking in the morning, a perfect army of doubts clamoring at my door for admittance. I have been compelled to lift up the "shield of faith" the moment I have become conscious of these suggestions of doubt, and handing the whole army over to the Lord to conquer, I have begun to assert, over and over, my faith in Him, in the simple words, "God is my Father; I am His forgiven child; He does love me; Jesus saves me; Jesus saves me now!" The victory is always complete. The enemy has come in like a flood, but the "Spirit of the Lord shall lift up a standard against him" (Isaiah 59:19 KJV), and my doubts have been put to flight. Dear doubting souls, go and do likewise, and a similar victory shall be yours. No earthly father has ever declared or shown his fatherhood a fraction as unmistakably or as lovingly as your heavenly Father has declared and shown His. If you would not "make God a liar," therefore, make your believing as inevitable and necessary a thing as your obedience.

LOVE GROWN DARK

Dwight Lyman Moody

When Jesus therefore saw his mother,
and the disciple standing by,
whom he loved, he saith unto his mother,
Woman, behold thy son!
John 19:26 KJV

A poor man sent his son to school in the city. The young man was walking down the street with two of his school friends. His father, who was hauling wood, saw him and went to the sidewalk to speak to him. But the boy was ashamed of his father and said, "I don't know you." Will such a young man ever amount to anything? Never!

I remember a very promising young man whom I had in Sunday school in Chicago. His mother took in washing to educate her four children. This was her eldest son, and I thought that he was going to redeem the whole family. One day he stood with his mother at the cottage door—it was a poor house because she could not pay for their schooling, feed and clothe her children, and rent a very good house, too. When they were talking, a young man from the high school came up the street. This boy walked away from his mother. The next day the young man asked, "Who was that I saw you talking to yesterday?"

He replied, "That was my washerwoman."

I thought, *Poor fellow! He will never amount to anything.* That was a good many years ago. He has gone down, down, down, and now he is just a miserable wreck. Of course he would go down. Ashamed of his mother who loved him and toiled for him and bore so much hardship for him!

WHAT WOULD JESUS DO—
THE BEAUTIFUL SINGER

Charles Sheldon

Because Christ also suffered for us,
leaving us an example,
that ye should follow his steps.
1 Peter 2:21 KJV

Of what Christian use was Rachel Winslow's talent of song? Was the best she could do to sell her talent for so much a month, go on a concert company's tour, dress beautifully, enjoy the excitement of public applause, and gain a reputation as a great singer? Was that what Jesus would do?

She said, "I have made up my mind to use my voice in some way so as to satisfy my own soul that I am doing something better than pleasing fashionable audiences or making money or even gratifying my own love of singing. I am going to do something that will satisfy me when I ask: 'What would Jesus do?' I am not satisfied and cannot be when I think of myself as singing myself into the career of a concert company performer.

"During the week I am going to sing at the White Cross meetings down in the Rectangle, the slum district. They use a tent. It is in a part of the city where Christian work is most needed. What have we done all our lives for the suffering, sinning side of the city of Raymond? How much have we denied ourselves or given of our personal ease and pleasure to bless the place in which we live or imitate the life of the Savior?"

Miss Winslow has chosen to give her great talent to the poor of the city. Her plans include a musical institute where choruses and classes in vocal music shall be a feature. She is enthusiastic over her lifework.

UNCHANGEABLE LOVE

GEORGE MÜLLER

*Now I beg you, brethren, through the Lord Jesus Christ,
and through the love of the Spirit, that you strive together
with me in prayers to God for me.*
ROMANS 15:30 NKJV

This evening I was walking in our little garden, meditating on the fact that Jesus Christ is the same yesterday, today, and forever. While meditating on His unchangeable love, power, and wisdom, I turned my meditation, as I went on, into prayer concerning myself. While applying likewise His unchangeable love, power, and wisdom both to my present spiritual and earthly circumstances—all at once the present need of the orphanage was brought to my mind. Immediately I was led to say to myself, "Jesus in His love and power has previously supplied me with what I have needed for the orphans. In the same unchangeable love and power, He will provide me with what I may need for the future." A flow of joy came into my soul while realizing the unchangeableness of our adorable Lord.

About one minute after, a letter was brought to me, enclosing an amount of money. In it was written: "Will you apply the amount of the enclosed money to the furtherance of the objects of your Scriptural Knowledge Society, or of your Orphan Establishment, or in the work and cause of our Master in any way that He Himself, on your application to Him, may point out to you. It is not a great sum, but it is a sufficient provision for the requirements of today." This money allowed me to meet the expenses of the orphanages that came upon me four days later.

AFFECTIONATE LOVE

DAVID LIVINGSTONE

*Surely your goodness and love will follow me all the days of my life,
and I will dwell in the house of the LORD forever.*
PSALM 23:6 NIV

Great pains had been taken by my parents to instill the doctrines of Christianity into my mind, and I had no difficulty in understanding the theory of our free salvation by the atonement of our Savior. I really began to feel the necessity and value of a personal application of the provisions of that atonement to my own case.

The change was like what may be supposed would take place were it possible to cure a case of "color blindness." The perfect freeness with which the pardon of all our guilt is offered in God's Book drew forth feelings of affectionate love to Him who bought us with His blood. A sense of deep obligation to Him for His mercy has influenced my conduct ever since. But I shall not again refer to the inner spiritual life, which I believe then began, nor do I intend to specify with any prominence the evangelistic labors to which the love of Christ has since impelled me. I will speak, not so much of what has been done, as of what still remains to be performed, before the Gospel can be said to be preached to all nations.

In the glow of love, which Christianity inspires, I soon resolved to devote my life to the alleviation of human misery. Turning this idea over in my mind, I therefore set myself to obtain a medical education, in order to be qualified for that enterprise.

HEAVEN'S LOVED INHABITANTS

DWIGHT LYMAN MOODY

Blessed the guest at home in your place!
We expect our fill of good things in your house,
your heavenly manse.
PSALM 65:4 MSG

If there is anything that ought to make heaven near to Christians, it is knowing that God and all their loved ones will be there. What is it that makes home so attractive? Is it because we have a beautiful house? Is it because we have beautiful lawns? Is it because we have beautiful trees around that home? Is it because we have beautiful paintings upon the walls inside? Is it because we have beautiful furniture? Is that all that makes home so attractive and so beautiful? No, it is the loved ones there.

I remember when after being away from home some time I went back to see my honored mother. I thought in going back I would take her by surprise and come in unexpectedly upon her. I went into one room and then into another, and I went all through the house, but I could not find that loved mother. When I was told she had gone away, the old place didn't seem like home at all. Home had lost its charm to me. It was my mother who made home so sweet to me. It is the loved ones who make home so sweet to everyone. It is the loved ones who are going to make heaven so sweet to all of us. Christ is there, God the Father is there, and many, many who were dear to us who lived on earth are there—and we shall be with them by and by.

LOVE AND EASY BURDENS

REUBEN ARCHER TORREY

For the love of God is this,
that we obey his commandments.
And his commandments are not burdensome.
1 JOHN 5:3 NRSV

I never knew anyone to come to Christ yet who did not have to give up something. But the only things God asks you to give up are the things that are doing you harm. God has given to each one of us a guarantee that He will never ask us to give up anything that is for our good, and that guarantee is His own Son. I do not think if God has given His Son to die for us, He is going to ask us to give up anything that is good for us.

I remember when once I was talking to a young lady about coming to Christ. She said, "Well, I would like to be a Christian. But there is too much to give up."

I said, "Do you think God loves you?"

"I know He does," she replied.

"How much do you think God loves you?"

"God loved me enough to give His Son to die for me," she said.

I said, "Do you think that God, if He loved you enough to give His Son to die for you, will ask you to give up anything that is good for you to keep?"

She said, "No, He will not."

I said, "Do you want to keep anything that is not for your highest good?"

She replied, "No."

"Then do you not think you would better come to Christ right now?"

She said, "I will," and she did.

LOVE FOR THE MULTITUDES

CHARLES SHELDON

But when he saw the multitudes,
he was moved with compassion on them,
because they fainted, and were scattered abroad,
as sheep having no shepherd.
MATTHEW 9:36 KJV

Maxwell rose to speak to a crowd in the tent. This time he felt calmer. What would Jesus do? He spoke as he thought once he never could speak. Who were these people? They were immortal souls. What was Christianity? A calling of sinners, not the righteous, to repentance. How would Jesus speak? What would He say? He could not tell all that His message would include, but he felt sure of a part of it. And in that certainty he spoke on.

Never before had he felt "compassion for the multitude." What had the multitude been to him during his ten years in the First Church but a vague, dangerous, dirty, troublesome factor in society, outside of the church and of his reach, an element that caused him occasionally an unpleasant twinge of conscience, a factor in the slum district of Raymond that was talked about as the "masses," in papers written by the brethren in attempts to show why the "masses" were not being reached. But tonight as he faced the masses, he asked himself whether after all this was not just about such a multitude as Jesus faced most often, and he felt the genuine emotion of love for a crowd, which is one of the best indications a preacher ever has that he is living close to the heart of the world's eternal Life. It is easy to love an individual sinner, especially if he is personally picturesque or interesting. To love a multitude of sinners is distinctively a Christlike quality.

NOBLE LOVE

Thomas à Kempis

These were more noble than those in Thessalonica,
in that they received the word with all readiness of mind,
and searched the scriptures daily,
whether those things were so.
Acts 17:11 KJV

Ah, Lord God, my holy Lover, when You come into my heart, all that is within me will rejoice. You are my glory and the exultation of my heart. You are my hope and refuge in the day of my tribulation. But because my love is as yet weak and my virtue imperfect, I must be strengthened and comforted by You. Visit me often, therefore, and teach me Your holy discipline. Free me from evil passions and cleanse my heart of all disorderly affection so that, healed and purified within, I may be fit to love, strong to suffer, and firm to persevere.

Love is an excellent thing, a very great blessing indeed. It makes every difficulty easy and bears all wrongs with composure. For it bears a burden without being weighted and renders sweet all that is bitter. The noble love of Jesus spurs to great deeds and excites longing for that which is more perfect. Love tends upward; it will not be held down by anything low. Love wishes to be free and estranged from all worldly affections lest its inward sight be obstructed, lest it be entangled in any transitory interest and overcome by adversity.

Nothing is sweeter than love, nothing stronger or higher or wider; nothing is more pleasant, nothing fuller, and nothing better in heaven or on earth, for love is born of God and cannot rest except in God who is above all created things.

REFORM SCHOOL BOYS

CHARLES FINNEY

*Whoever pursues righteousness and love
finds life, prosperity and honor.*
PROVERBS 21:21 NIV

A friend of mine was in charge of a reform school for boys. The effects produced on even the worst boys by the love shown them are really striking. The superintendent had long insisted that he did not want locks and bars to confine his boys. On one occasion the superintendent was to be absent two weeks. A director came to him urging that he must lock up the boys before he left for they would certainly run away. The superintendent replied, "I think not; I have confidence in those boys."

"But," responded the director, "give us some guarantee. Are you willing to pledge that if they do run away, your city lot goes to the reform school fund?"

After a little reflection he consented. "I will give you my lot—all the little property I have in the world—if any of my boys run away while I am gone."

He called all the boys together, explained to them his pledge, and asked them to look at his dependent family. He then appealed to their honor and their love for him. "Would you be willing to see me stripped of all my property? I think I can trust you."

He went and returned a little unexpectedly and late on one Saturday night. Scarce had he entered the yard when the word rang through the sleeping halls, "Our father has come!" and almost in a moment they were there greeting him and shouting, "We are all here! We are all here!"

Cannot Christ's love have as much power as that?

LOVE AND LANGUAGE

Dwight Lyman Moody

Out of the same mouth proceedeth blessing and cursing.
My brethren, these things ought not so to be.
James 3:10 KJV

People often ask, "How can I keep from swearing?" I will tell you. If God puts His love into your heart, you will have no desire to curse Him. I was preaching one day in the open air, when a man drove up in a fine carriage, and after listening a little while, he put the whip to his fine-looking steed, and away he went.

Later, I visited him at his home. "I am told that God has blessed you above all men in this part of the country. He has given you wealth, a beautiful Christian wife, and seven lovely children. I do not know if it is true, but I hear that all He gets in return is cursing and blasphemy."

The man said, "What you say is true. But you don't know anything about a businessman's troubles. When he is harassed and tormented the whole time, he can't help swearing."

"Yes," I said, "he can. I used to swear myself." I began to tell him about Christ in the heart and how that would take the temptation to swear out of a man. At the next church prayer meeting, the man was there. He said, "My friends, I want to have you pray for my salvation."

Thirty-odd years later I spoke to the man. He said, "I have never had a desire to swear since then. It was all taken away." He was not only converted but became an earnest, active Christian and all these years has been serving God.

LOVE WITHOUT DOUBT

Hannah Whitall Smith

*For the one who doubts is like a wave of the sea,
driven and tossed by the wind.*
James 1:6 NRSV

I knew one devoted Christian whose religious life was one long torment of doubt. He thought that perfect confidence could only arise from a feeling that he was good enough to be worthy of God's love, but he felt this would be presumptive. But our confidence does not come from our own goodness but from the goodness of God. While we never can be and never ought to be satisfied with goodness in ourselves, there cannot possibly be any question to one who believes the Bible as to the all-sufficiency of God's goodness.

A wavering Christian is a Christian who trusts in the love of God one day and doubts it the next, and who is alternately happy or miserable. He mounts to the hilltop of joy at one time, only to descend at another time into the valley of despair. He is driven to and fro by every wind of doctrine, is always striving and never attaining, and is a prey to each changing influence, caused by his state of health or by the influences around him or even by the state of the weather.

If you believe one day that God loves you and is favorable to you and the next day doubt His love and fear that He is angry with you, does it not stand to reason that you must waver in your experience from joy to misery? Only a steadfast faith in His love and care could give you an unwavering experience.

INSEPARABLE LOVE

John Wycliffe

Many waters cannot quench love;
rivers cannot sweep it away.
If one were to give all the wealth of one's house for love,
it would be utterly scorned.
Song of Solomon 8:7 niv

Love is inseparable when a man's mind is inflamed with great love and clings to Christ by inseparable thought. Such a man does not allow Christ to be any moment out of his mind. As though he were bound in the heart, he thinks upon and draws his spirit from God. Therefore, the love of Christ so grows in the heart of the lover of God and despiser of the world that it may not be overcome by any other affection or love. When a man clings to Christ continuously, thinking upon Him, forgetting Him for no other occasion, then man's love is said to be inseparable and everlasting.

Love moves a soul in which it dwells to sing of his beloved. Love unites the lover and the beloved. Love is the desire of the heart, ever thinking on that which it loves. Love is a stirring of the soul to love God for Himself and all other things for God. This love puts out all other love that is against God's will. Love is a right will, turned from all earthly things, and joined to God without departing, accompanied with the fire of the Holy Spirit.

In this manner shall a lover of Jesus Christ be. He shall so burn in love that he shall be wholly turned into the fire of love. He shall so shine in virtues that no part of him will be dark in vices.

CHRISTIAN WORK REQUIRES LOVE

ANDREW MURRAY

There is no fear in love;
but perfect love casteth out fear.
1 JOHN 4:18 KJV

Love is the only power in which Christians really can do their work. Love is a fire that will burn through every difficulty. You may be a shy, hesitating person who cannot speak well, but love can burn through everything. A lady had been asked to speak at a rescue mission where there were a number of poor women. As she entered, she saw a woman sitting outside in deplorable condition and asked, "Who is that?"

The female supervisor answered, "She has been into the house thirty or forty times, and she has always gone away again. Nothing can be done with her. We have been waiting for you, and you have only an hour for your speech."

The lady replied, "No, this is of more importance." She went outside where the woman was sitting and said, "My sister, what is the matter?"

"I am not your sister" was the reply.

Then the lady laid her hand on her and said, "Yes, I am your sister, and I love you." She so spoke until the heart of the poor woman was touched. The conversation lasted some time, and those inside were waiting patiently. Ultimately the lady brought the woman into the room. She would not sit on a chair but sat down on a stool beside the speaker's seat. And that love touched the woman's heart. She had found one who really loved her, and that love gave access to the love of Jesus. I plead that God would begin with us now and baptize us with heavenly love!

LOVE OF MONEY

Reuben Archer Torrey

For the love of money is a root of all kinds of evil,
and in their eagerness to be rich some have wandered away
from the faith and pierced themselves with many pains.
1 Timothy 6:10 NRSV

The love of money keeps many men from coming to Christ. Many a man knows that if he came to Christ he would lose money by it. There are things in his business that would need to be given up. But he is not willing to sacrifice the profits he gets in crooked ways. He is deliberately choosing a larger income and eternal death instead of Jesus Christ and eternal life.

How many a young fellow has come to me, and when I have urged him to come to Christ, he has said, "I believe it is a good thing, but I should have to give up my employment if I did."

Two young ladies said to Mrs. Torrey, when they seemed to be very near a decision, "We cannot come to Christ. We are employed in a large shop, and our employer requires us to misrepresent the goods. We cannot do that and be Christians, can we?"

"No, you cannot," Mrs. Torrey replied, and the young ladies said, "If we don't, then we lose our positions." God pity the man or the merchant who requires his employees to lie! How sad it is that those young women were ready to choose their position and small salary in the place of Jesus Christ and life eternal!

REDEEM TIME FOR LOVE

JOHN WESLEY

*So he [Paul] reasoned in the synagogue with both Jews
and God-fearing Greeks, as well as in the marketplace
day by day with those who happened to be there.*
ACTS 17:17 NIV

Monday, August 22, 1743 (London)—After a few of us
had joined in prayer, about four o'clock I set out and rode
easily to Snow Hill, where, the saddle slipping quite upon
my mare's neck, I fell over her head, and she ran back into
Smithfield. Some boys caught her and brought her to me
again, cursing and swearing all the way. I spoke plainly to
them, and they promised to amend their ways.

I was setting forward when a man cried, "Sir, you have
lost your saddlecloth." Two or three more came to help me
put it on, but these, too, swore at almost every word. I turned
to one and another and spoke in love. They all took it well
and thanked me much. I gave them two or three little books,
which they promised to read over carefully.

Before I reached Kensington, I found my mare had lost
a shoe. This gave me an opportunity of talking closely for
nearly half an hour both to the blacksmith and his assistant.
I mention these little circumstances to show how easy it is to
redeem every fragment of time (if I may so speak) when we
feel any love to those souls for which Christ died.

LOVE OF IDOLS

REUBEN ARCHER TORREY

*"You shall not make for yourself an image
in the form of anything in heaven above
or on the earth beneath or in the waters below.
You shall not bow down to them or worship them."*
EXODUS 20:4–5 NIV

What is an idol? An idol is anything that takes the place of God. It is anything that is the supreme object of our affection. God alone has the right to the supreme place in our hearts. Everything and everyone else must be subordinate to Him.

Many a man makes an idol of his wife. Not that a man can love his wife any too much, but he can put her in the wrong place. He can put her before God. When a man regards his wife's pleasure before God's pleasure, when he gives her the first place and God the second place, his wife is an idol.

Many a woman makes an idol of her children. Not that we can love our children too much. The more dearly we love Christ, the more dearly we love our children, but we can put our children in the wrong place. We can put them before God and their interests before God's interests. When we do this, our children are our idols.

Many a man makes an idol of his reputation or his business. Reputation or business is put before God.

One great question for us to decide: Is God absolutely first? Is He before wife, before children, before reputation, before business, before our own lives?

Improving Your Love Life:

Radical Ways to Inspire Others

THE SWORD OF LOVE

GILBERT K. CHESTERTON

*Love prospers when a fault is forgiven;
but dwelling on it separates close friends.*
PROVERBS 17:9 NLT

Can a person hate the world enough to change it, and yet love it enough to think it worth changing? Can he look up at its colossal evil without feeling despair? I want to love my neighbor not because he is I, but precisely because he is not I. I want to adore the world, not as a person likes looking at his image in a mirror because it is one's self, but as one loves a woman because she is entirely different. If souls are separate, love is possible. A man may be said loosely to love himself, but he can hardly fall in love with himself.

And it is just here that Christianity is on the side of humanity, liberty, and love. Love desires personality; therefore, love desires differences. It is the instinct of Christianity to be glad that God has broken the universe into little pieces, because they are living pieces. It is Christianity's innate nature to say "Little children love one another," rather than to tell one large person to love himself.

Christianity is a sword that separates and sets free. No other philosophy makes God actually rejoice in the separation of the universe into living souls. But according to Christianity, this separation between God and man is sacred, because this is eternal. For a person to love God, it is necessary that there should be not only a God to be loved but a person to love Him.

TEACHING CHILDREN LOVE

JOHN HENRY JOWETT

*[Jesus] said to them, "Let the little children come to me,
and do not hinder them, for the kingdom of God
belongs to such as these."*
MARK 10:14 NIV

To win a child's love and admiration and hope is to grip his entire being and conquer all the powers of his soul. If Jesus, the great Lover, can win these, the pursuit will be followed by the wedding. How can we so represent Him that this triumph shall be won?

We live by love. By admiration, too! Our children must not only find in Jesus their Savior; they must find in Him their hero, too. Say to yourself, "I will so present my Master as a hero as to attract the adoring homage of my children." Would you be without any heroic subject matter? Your eyes are closed and sealed if you do not see the heroic glowing upon every page of the sacred story! His splendid bravery; His tremendous hatred of all meanness and sin; His magnificent solitude in the night; His strenuous refusal of a popular crown, when the sovereignty would mean compromise with the powers of darkness! Let these be unfolded with the same tremendous effort and vivid realization that we make when we seek to unveil the heroism of earthly achievers, and our boys and girls will go on their knees before the unveiling with reverent admiration and homage.

The glorious Lord will become the children's staff of life. Their worship will become their desire. Their loving will become their longing. Their admiration will become aspiration. Their faith will become their hope.

STAND ON LOVE

F. B. MEYER

Don't just pretend to love others. Really love them.
Hate what is wrong. Hold tightly to what is good.
ROMANS 12:9 NLT

The prophet Nehemiah had a perfect right to take tax money from the people, but he did not. Not a word could be said even by his critics, if he did. He was doing a priceless work and might justly claim his support. On the other hand, the people were very poor, and he would have a larger influence over them if he were prepared to stand on their level and to share with them.

Often we must forego our evident rights and liberties in order to influence others for Christ. Do not always stand on your rights. Instead, live for others, making any sacrifice in order to save some—even as Christ loved us and gave Himself for us. What ought we to do for love? Love is more relentless than law. Its demands are more stringent and searching. Are we doing as much for love of Jesus as generations before did simply out of duty? But what Jesus does get is infinitely sweet to Him insofar as love prompts it.

All around you, people are doing things that they say are perfectly legitimate. They call you narrow-minded and bigoted because you do not join with them. They are always arguing with you in an effort to prove you are wrong. But your supreme law is your attitude to your Master: "I cannot do otherwise for the love of Jesus."

GROWING IN FAITH

CHARLES FINNEY

He has shown you, O mortal, what is good.
And what does the LORD require of you?
To act justly and to love mercy
and to walk humbly with your God.
MICAH 6:8 NIV

Think how grieved and alarmed you would be if you discovered any ebbing of affection for you in your wife, husband, or children, if you saw another engrossing their hearts and thoughts and time. Perhaps in such a case you would well nigh die with a just and virtuous jealousy. Now, God calls Himself a jealous God, and have you not given your heart to other loves and infinitely offended Him?

Growth in the knowledge of God is a condition of growth in His favor. We might grow in knowledge without growing in His favor, because we might not love and trust Him in accordance with the increased knowledge. We cannot love and trust Him more perfectly, unless we become more perfectly acquainted with Him. If our love and faith keep pace with our growing knowledge, we must grow in His favor. But growth in knowledge must be a condition of growth in love and faith.

When we are more and more affected by the mercies of God and by the kindnesses of those around us, when we more thoroughly appreciate manifestations of kindness in God, when we are more and more humbled by these kindnesses and find it more and more natural "to act justly and to love mercy and to walk humbly," and live gratefully, we have evidence that we are growing in favor with God.

CHARITY MEANS LOVE

George Whitefield

Love never fails.
But whether there are prophecies, they will fail;
whether there are tongues, they will cease;
whether there is knowledge, it will vanish away.
1 Corinthians 13:8 NKJV

Nothing is more valuable and commendable, and yet not one duty is less practiced than that of charity. But before I go any further, I shall inform you what the apostle means by charity, and that is love. If there is true love, there will be charity. There will be an endeavor to assist, help, and relieve according to that ability wherewith God has blessed us.

We often pretend concern for the misery of our fellow creatures, but yet we seldom commiserate their condition so much as to relieve them according to our abilities. But unless we assist them with what they may stand in need of—for the body as well as for the soul—all our wishes are no more than words of no value. When we hear of any deplorable circumstance in which our fellow creatures are involved, be they friends or enemies, it is our duty as Christians to assist them to the utmost of our power.

Saint Paul had been showing that spiritual gifts were diverse. Though there are these different spiritual gifts, they are all given for some wise end. We are not to hide those gifts that God has given us. They are to be used for the glory of God and the good of immortal souls. After he had particularly illustrated this, Saint Paul comes to show that all gifts, however great they may be in themselves, are of no value unless we have charity.

THE STRENGTH FOR LOVE

WILLIAM TYNDALE

I love you, O Lord, my strength.
PSALM 18:1 NRSV

The law requires a free, a willing, and a loving heart. I may of my own strength refrain from hurting my enemy, but to love him with all my heart and put anger out of my mind, I cannot do of my own strength. I may refuse money of my own strength, but to put away love for riches out of my heart, I cannot do of my own strength. To abstain from adultery, as concerning the outward deed, I can do of my own strength; but not to desire in my heart is as impossible to me as to choose whether I will hunger or thirst. Yet the law requires it. Of our own strength the law is never fulfilled. We must have God's favor and His Spirit, purchased by Christ's blood.

Love of her own nature bestows all that she has, and even her own self, on that which is loved. You need not remind a kind mother to be loving unto her only son. Much less does spiritual love, which has eyes given to her by God, need human law to teach her to do her duty.

We should deal soberly with the consciences of the weak in faith, who do not yet understand the liberty of Christ perfectly enough. Favor them with Christian love, and do not use the liberty of faith as a hindrance, but use it to edify the weak. Where love is perfect, there must be such a respect for the weak. It is a thing that Christ commanded and charged to be had above all things.

LOVE FOR THE UNLOVELY

Andrew Murray

But as touching brotherly love
ye need not that I write unto you:
for ye yourselves are taught of God
to love one another.
1 Thessalonians 4:9 kjv

It is in our daily life and conduct that the fruit of the Spirit is love. From that comes all the graces and virtues in which love is manifested. I have often thought that if we had written this we would have put in the foreground the manly virtues, such as zeal, courage, and diligence. But we need to see how the gentler virtues—kindness, humbleness, meekness, and long-suffering—are specially connected with dependence upon the Holy Spirit. They never were found in the heathen world. Christ was needed to come from heaven to teach them to us.

I cannot see God, but as a compensation I can see my brother. If I love him, God dwells in me. Loving my brother is the way to real fellowship with God. Suppose there is a brother, a most unlovable man. He worries you every time you meet him. He is of the very opposite disposition to yours. You have to deal with him in your business. He is most untidy and unbusinesslike. You say, "I cannot love him." Friend, you have not learned the lesson that Christ wanted to teach above everything. Let a man be what he will; you are to love him. Yes, listen! If a man loves not his brother whom he hath seen—if you don't love that unlovable man whom you have seen—how can you love God whom you have not seen? If the love of God is in your heart, you will love your brother.

LOVE LIKE CHRIST

Hannah Whitall Smith

For the love of Christ urges us on,
because we are convinced that one has died for all;
therefore all have died.
2 Corinthians 5:14 nrsv

Seeing God in everything will make us loving and patient with those who annoy and trouble us. They will be to us then only the means for accomplishing His tender and wise purposes toward us. We shall even find ourselves at last inwardly thanking them for the blessings they bring us.

If our Father permits a trial to come, it must be because that trial is the best thing that could happen to us. We must accept it with thanks from His dear hand. The trial itself may be hard upon us, and I do not mean that we can enjoy the suffering of it. But we can and must love the will of God in the trial because His will is always sweet, whether it be in joy or in sorrow.

If you are really one with Christ, you will be sweet to those who are cross to you. You will bear everything and make no complaints. When you are reviled, you will not revile again and feel nothing but love in return. You will seek the honor of others rather than your own. You will take the lowest place and be the servant of all, as Christ was. You will literally and truly love your enemies and do good to them who despitefully use you. You will, in short, live a Christlike life and show outwardly—as well as feel inwardly—a Christlike spirit. This is what it is to be one with Christ.

ZEAL AND LOVE

Jeremy Taylor

But since you excel in everything—
in faith, in speech, in knowledge,
in complete earnestness and in the love we have kindled in you—
see that you also excel in this grace of giving.
2 Corinthians 8:7 NIV

Love must be obedient, pure, simple, and communicative; that is, it must be expressive. However, zeal must come after a long growth of a temperate and well-regulated love. That zeal only is good which in a fervent love has temperate expressions. For let the affection boil as high as it can, yet if it boils over into irregular and strange actions, it will need many excuses. Moses broke the tablets of the law by being passionately zealous against them who broke the first commandment.

Zeal must spend its greatest heat principally in those things that concern ourselves but with great care and restraint in those that concern others. Remember that zeal must in no sense contradict any action of love. Love to God includes love to our neighbor, and therefore no pretence of zeal for God's glory must make us uncharitable to our brother. Doing so is as pleasing to God as hatred is an act of love. Zeal directed to others can spend itself in nothing but charitable actions for their good.

Let loose zeal in matters of internal, personal, and spiritual actions that are matters of direct duty such as prayers and thanksgiving. Zeal is only acceptable and safe when it advances the love of God and our neighbors. In brief, let your zeal (if it must be expressed in anger) be always more severe against yourself than against others.

LEARNING LOVE

Henry Drummond

From him the whole body,
joined and held together by every supporting ligament,
grows and builds itself up in love, as each part does its work.
Ephesians 4:16 niv

To learn love is the supreme work to which we need to address ourselves in this world. Is life not full of opportunities for learning love? Every man and woman every day has a thousand of them. The world is not a playground; it is a schoolroom. Life is not a holiday but an education. The one eternal lesson for us all is how better we can love. What makes a person a good ball player? Practice. What makes a person a good artist, a good sculptor, a good musician? Practice. What makes a person a good person? Practice. Nothing else.

If a man does not exercise his arm, he develops no biceps muscle; and if a man does not exercise his soul, he acquires no muscle in his soul, no strength of character, no vigor of moral fiber nor beauty of spiritual growth. Love is a rich, strong, and vigorous expression of the whole round Christian character—the Christlike nature in its fullest development. And the components of this great character are only to be built up by ceaseless practice. What was Christ doing in the carpenter's shop? Practicing. Though perfect, we read that He learned obedience, and He increased in wisdom and in favor with God and man.

Talent develops itself in solitude—the talent of prayer, of faith, of meditation, of seeing the unseen. Character grows in the stream of the world's life. That chiefly is where we are to learn love.

THE BRIDEGROOM'S FRIENDS

GEORGE WHITEFIELD

In love of the brethren be tenderly affectioned one to another;
in honor preferring one another.
ROMANS 12:10 ASV

If we are married to Jesus Christ, we shall not only reverence the bridegroom, but we shall also love and honor the bridegroom's friends. Jesus says, "By this shall all men know that ye are my disciples, if ye have love one to another" (John 13:35 KJV).

"By this we know," says the beloved disciple, "that we have passed from death unto life, because we love the brethren" (1 John 3:14 KJV). Observe love for the brethren without limit of whatever denomination. This was the case of the primitive Christians. They were all of one heart and of one mind. It was said of them (Oh, that it could be said of us!): "See how these Christians love one another!"

They were of the same spirit as a good woman of Scotland who saw a great multitude coming from various parts to receive the blessed sacrament. She saluted them with a "Come in, ye blessed of the Lord, I have a house that will hold a hundred of you, and a heart that will hold ten thousand." Let us go and do likewise. . . .

If we are married to Jesus Christ, we shall be willing to bear His cross as well as to wear His crown. They will cry out, "Crown Him, crown Him," when others are crying out, "Crucify Him, crucify Him."

THE MEASURE OF LOVE

JEREMY TAYLOR

And this is love: that we walk in obedience to his commands.
As you have heard from the beginning,
his command is that you walk in love.
2 JOHN 1:6 NIV

We must be careful that our love to God is sweet, even, and full of tranquillity, having in it no violence. A new beginner in religion has passionate desires. But they must not be the measure of his actions. He must consider his spiritual strength and not go to storm a strong fort or attack a potent enemy or do heroic actions that are fit for giants in religion. Indiscreet and untimely actions are the rocks of religion against which tender spirits often suffer shipwreck.

Let our love be prudent and without illusion so that it expresses itself in such instances which God has chosen or which we choose ourselves by proportion to His rules and measures. Love turns into doting when religion turns into superstition. No degree of love can be imprudent, but the expressions may. We cannot love God too much, but we may proclaim it in an indecent manner.

Let our love be firm, constant, and inseparable. Let it not be coming and returning like the tide, but descending like a never-failing river, ever running into the ocean of divine excellency, passing on in the channels of duty and a constant obedience. Let our love never cease to be what it is until it is turned into sea and vastness, even the immensity of a blessed eternity.

DO IT FOR LOVE

F. B. MEYER

Act with love and justice,
and always depend on him.
HOSEA 12:6 NLT

The man who does his business with all his heart is sure to prosper. It is a great thing to love our lifework and to have an aim that kindles us to action whenever we think of it. Those who are happy in their circumstances cannot be sufficiently thankful. But what of those who are bound to a work that they did not choose and do not like, who find their daily toil irksome and distasteful—is there any help for them? Can they possibly learn to do such work from their hearts? Certainly: because of Him who set it and for whom it may be done.

Love performs the most onerous duties with all its heart if they advance the comfort and help of those whom it loves more than itself. A mother or wife performs tasks from which the hired person would shrink. She does them with all her heart, not considering for a moment the disagreeableness and hardness of the demand. So if we look at our lifework as appointed by God, if we can hear the voice of Jesus saying, "Do this for Me," there is no further thought of hardship or distaste. Remember to do all your lifework for Jesus. Do all in His name and for His glory. Ask Him to fill your heart with submissive, loyal obedience. You will find that when you introduce the personal element of service to Christ into the most ordinary acts, they will glisten like a piece of gold tapestry.

THE NATURE OF CHRIST'S LOVE

JOHN BUNYAN

For I am not ashamed of the gospel;
it is the power of God for salvation
to everyone who has faith, to the Jew first
and also to the Greek.
ROMANS 1:16 NRSV

I will present these things as helps to the knowledge of the nature of the love of Christ and helps to retain it. First, you cannot know the love of Christ before you know the badness of your nature. He who sees but little of his sinful nature will hardly know much of the love of Christ. He who sees of himself nothing at all will hardly ever see anything of the love of Christ. But he who sees most of what a miserable character he is, he is likely to see most of what is the love of Christ. So then if a man would be kept sure and steadfast, let him labor before all things to know his own wretchedness.

Labor to see the emptiness, shortness, and pollution that clings to a man's own righteousness. This also must in some measure be known before a man can know the nature of the love of Christ.

To know the nature of Christ's love, be much in acquainting yourself with the nature of the law and the nature of the Gospel. The law is a servant, both first and last, to the Gospel. For there is nothing that Satan more desires than that the law may take the place of Christ and faith.

INTERCEDE IN LOVE

George Whitefield

I exhort therefore, first of all,
that supplications, prayers, intercessions,
thanksgivings, be made for all men.
1 Timothy 2:1 asv

If we inquire why there is so little love to be found among Christians, we shall find it owing to a neglect of that excellent part of prayer: intercession—imploring divine grace and mercy on behalf of others.

Some forget this duty of praying for others because they seldom remember to pray for themselves. Even those who are constant in praying to their Father are often so selfish in their addresses that they do not enlarge their petitions for the welfare of their fellow Christians.

Intercession will fill your hearts with love one to another. He who every day heartily intercedes at the throne of grace for all mankind cannot but in a short time be filled with love and charity to all. The frequent exercise of his love in this manner will gradually enlarge his heart. He will be filled with joy, peace, meekness, long-suffering, and all other graces of the Holy Spirit. By frequently laying his neighbor's wants before God, he will be touched with a fellow-feeling for them. Every blessing bestowed on others, instead of exciting envy in him, will be looked on as an answer to his particular intercession and fill his soul with joy unspeakable and full of glory.

Abound therefore in acts of general and particular intercessions. You cannot imagine what a blessed alteration this practice will make in your heart and how much you will increase day by day in the spirit of love and meekness toward all mankind!

DEEPER LOVE

JOHN CALVIN

Continue your love to those who know you,
your righteousness to the upright in heart.
PSALM 36:10 NIV

Jesus says, "As the Father has loved Me, so have I loved You: Continue in My love." There is much more to this statement than is commonly believed. It was Christ's purpose to deposit in our laps a sure pledge of God's love toward us. The love in question here has to do with us because it is as the head of the church that Christ testifies to God's love for Him. Let us fix our eyes on Christ because in Him we see the pledge of God's love clearly exhibited. God poured His love upon Him so that it might flow from Him to the members of His body. This is also the significance of the title "the beloved Son, in whom the will of the Father is satisfied." We must consider the purpose of this love, which is that God in Christ may be well pleased with us. Christ was loved by the Father not in and for Himself alone, but that He might with Himself unite us with the Father.

Some explain the words "Continue ye in my love" (John 15:9 KJV) to mean that Christ decreed for His disciples to love one another. He in fact bids us live always in the joy of the love with which He once and for all loved us, warning us not to deprive ourselves of it. Many reject the grace offered them. Once we are beneficiaries of the grace of Christ, let us see to it that we do not fall away from it through our own fault.

ADVICE ON PRAYER

ELIZABETH PRENTISS

Now devote your heart and soul to seeking the LORD your God. Begin to build the sanctuary of the LORD God, so that you may bring the ark of the covenant of the LORD and the sacred articles belonging to God into the temple that will be built for the Name of the LORD.

1 CHRONICLES 22:19 NIV

It is not necessary to say much to God. Oftentimes one does not speak much to a friend whom one is delighted to see; one looks at him with pleasure; one speaks certain short words to him that are mere expressions of feeling. The mind has no part in them, or next to none; one keeps repeating the same words. It is not so much a variety of thoughts that one seeks in intercourse with a friend as a certain repose and correspondence of heart. It is thus we are with God, who does not disdain to be our tenderest, most cordial, most familiar, most intimate friend. A word, a sigh, a sentiment says all to God; it is not always necessary to have transports of sensible tenderness; a will all naked and dry, without life, without vivacity, without pleasure is often purest in the sight of God. In fine, it is necessary to content one's self with giving to Him what He gives it to give, a fervent heart when it is fervent, a heart firm and faithful in its aridity, when He deprives it of sensible fervor. It does not always depend on you to feel; but it is necessary to wish to feel. Leave it to God to choose to make you feel sometimes in order to sustain your weakness and infancy in the Christian life; sometimes weaning you from that sweet and consoling sentiment that is the milk of babes, in order to humble you, to make you grow, and to make you robust in the violent exercise of faith, by causing you to eat the bread of the strong in the sweat of your brow. Would you only love God according as He will make you take pleasure in loving Him? You would be loving your own tenderness and feeling, fancying that you were loving God. Even while receiving sensible gifts, prepare yourself by pure faith for the time when you might be deprived of them; and you will suddenly succumb if you had only relied on such support.

I forgot to speak of some practices that may, at the beginning, facilitate the remembrances of the offering one ought to make to God of all the ordinary acts of the day.

1. Form the resolution to do so every morning, and call yourself to account in your self-examination at night.

2. Make no resolutions but for good reasons, either from propriety or the necessity of relaxing the mind, etc. Thus, in accustoming oneself to retrench the useless little by little, one accustoms oneself to offer to curtail what is not proper.

3. Renew oneself in this disposition whenever one is alone in order to be better prepared to recollect it when in company.

4. Whenever one surprises oneself in too great dissipation or in speaking too freely of his neighbor, let him collect himself and offer to God all the rest of the conversation.

5. Flee with confidence to God, acting according to His will when one enters company or engages in some occupation that may cause one to fall into temptation. The sight of danger ought to warn of the need there is to lift the heart toward Him by whom one may be preserved from it.

LOVE BALANCES THE SCALE

Reuben Archer Torrey

*"You have been weighed on the scales
and found wanting."*
DANIEL 5:27 NIV

Weighed by the laws of God, are you found wanting? One day I was talking to a sea captain. I asked, "Captain, why are you not a Christian?"

"The Golden Rule is a good enough religion for me," he replied.

"Do you keep it?" I asked. He dropped his head. He talked about it, but he did not keep it. Notice that scripture does not merely put the Golden Rule negatively: "Do not do to others whatsoever you would not that they should do to you." The Christian rule is positive. "Do these things to them." Do you do it? Always? Then you are weighed and found wanting.

In Matthew, the Bible tells us to love the Lord our God with all our heart, with all our soul, and with all our mind. This is the first and greatest commandment. How much do you weigh by that law? Put God first in everything—in business, in politics, in social life, in study, in everything. Do you do it? Have you always done it? No, you say, I have not. Then you are weighed and found wanting.

Every one of us is weighed and found wanting. What shall we do then? This is where the Gospel comes in. God has weighed the whole world in the balance and found it wanting. In Christ He provided salvation for a wanting world. When we take Christ into the balance with us, then we are weighed and found not wanting.

LOVE AND DISCIPLINE

CHARLES HADDON SPURGEON

"Those whom I love I rebuke and discipline.
So be earnest and repent."
REVELATION 3:19 NIV

Christ will have His favored church walk with great care, and if she will not follow Him fully by being shown wherein she has erred and will not repent when kindly counseled, He then takes some sharper means.

It is a very solemn thing to be dearly loved by God. It is a privilege to be coveted. But the person who is so honored occupies a position of great delicacy. The Lord your God is a jealous God, and He is most jealous where He shows most love. If the Lord gives a church a special blessing, He expects more of it—more care of His honor and more zeal for His glory. When He does not find it, what will happen? Because of His very love, He will rebuke it with hard sermons, sharp words, and painful blows to the conscience.

The chastening is a blessing and a token of love. Sorrow is often brought upon Christians by the sins of their fellow members. Many brothers and sisters love the Lord and want to see souls converted, but they can only sigh and cry because nothing is done. They are the ones who bear the burden of a lukewarm church.

The best remedy for churches in relapse is increased spiritual fellowship with Christ. Christ is outside the church, driven there by her unkindness, but He has not gone far away; He loves His church too much to leave her altogether. He longs to come back, and therefore He waits and knocks at the door.

WALKING IN GOD'S LOVE

GEORGE WHITEFIELD

And Enoch walked with God:
and he was not;
for God took him.
GENESIS 5:24 KJV

Walking with God implies our making progress or advances in the divine life. Walking, in the very first idea of the word, seems to suppose a progressive motion. A person who walks, though he moves slowly, yet he goes forward and does not continue in one place. So it is with those who walk with God.

In one sense, the divine life admits of neither increase nor decrease. When a soul is born of God, to all intents and purposes he is a child of God. Though he should live to the age of Methuselah, yet he would then be only a child of God after all. But in another sense, the divine life admits of decays and additions. Hence, it is that we find the people of God charged with backslidings and losing their first love.

Believers keep up and maintain their walk with God by reading His holy Word. "Search the scriptures," says our blessed Lord, "for these are they that testify of Me." If we cease making the written Word of God our sole rule both as to faith and practice, we shall soon lie open to all manner of delusion and be in great danger of making shipwreck of faith and a good conscience.

If you would walk with God, you will associate and keep company with those who do walk with Him. The primitive Christians, no doubt, kept up their vigor and first love by continuing in fellowship one with another.

REST IN FAITH

Hannah Whitall Smith

Return to your rest, my soul, for the LORD has been good to you.
PSALM 116:7 NIV

It [is] possible to obey God's commandment contained in [these] words, "Be careful for nothing; but in every thing by prayer and supplication with thanksgiving let your requests be made known unto God" (Philippians 4:6 KJV); and that in obeying it, the result would inevitably be, according to the promise, that the "peace of God, which passeth all understanding, shall keep your hearts and minds through Christ Jesus" (Philippians 4:7 KJV).

The soul who has discovered this secret of simple faith has found the key that will unlock the whole treasure-house of God.

Some child of God who is hungering for just such a life as I have been describing is reading this book. You long unspeakably to get rid of your weary burdens. You would be delighted to hand over the management of your unmanageable self into the hands of One who is able to manage you. Do you recollect the delicious sense of rest with which you have sometimes gone to bed at night after a day of great exertion and weariness? How delightful was the sensation of relaxing every muscle and letting your body go in a perfect abandonment of ease and comfort! You no longer had to hold up an aching head or a weary back. You trusted yourself to the bed in absolute confidence, and it held you up, without effort or strain or even thought on your part. You rested!

Suppose you had doubted the strength or the stability of your bed and had dreaded each moment to find it giving way beneath you and landing you on the floor. Could you have rested then? Would not every muscle have been strained in a fruitless effort to hold yourself up, and would not the weariness have been greater than if you had not gone to bed at all?

Let this analogy teach you what it means to rest in the Lord. Let your souls lie down upon the couch of His sweet will, as your bodies lie down in their beds at night. Relax every strain, and lay off every burden. Let yourself go in a perfect abandonment of ease and comfort, sure that, since He holds you up, you are perfectly safe. Your part is simply to rest. His part is to sustain you, and He cannot fail.

GROW IN LOVE

THOMAS WATSON

*Let them give thanks to the LORD for his unfailing love
and his wonderful deeds for mankind, for he satisfies the thirsty
and fills the hungry with good things.*
PSALM 107:8–9 NIV

Let me exhort Christians to increase your love to God. Let your love be raised up higher. Our love to God should be as the light of the morning: first there is the daybreak, then it shines brighter at noon. They who have a few sparks of love should fan those divine sparks into a flame. He who has a little gold would have more; you who love God a little, labor to love Him more. A godly man is contented with a very little of the world, yet he labors to add one degree of love to another.

When I see the almond tree bud and flourish, I know there is life in the root. Where we see love for God increasing and growing larger, we may conclude it is true and genuine. The disciples' love for Christ at first was weak; they fled from Christ. But after Christ's death, love grew more vigorous, and the disciples made an open declaration of Him.

If our love to God does not increase, it will soon decrease. If the fire is not stoked, it will quickly go out. Therefore Christians should above all things endeavor to cherish and excite their love to God. This encouragement will be out of date when we go to heaven, for then our light shall be clear and our love perfect; but now it is time to motivate ourselves so that our love for God may increase yet more and more.

LOVE WITHOUT DELAY

RICHARD BAXTER

It is good to. . .
declare your steadfast love in the morning,
and your faithfulness by night.
PSALM 92:1–2 NRSV

Enter upon saving souls with the right intentions. Aim at the glory of God in the person's salvation. Do it not to get a name for yourself or to bring people to depend upon you. Do it in obedience to Christ and in imitation of Him. Extend His tender love to people's souls.

Do not delay. While you are making ready to teach a person, sin is taking root, and temptations to sin multiply. Conscience grows seared, and the heart becomes hardened. Christ is shut out. Time runs on. Death and judgment are at the door. What if the person dies while you are getting ready! A physician is no better than a murderer who negligently delays until his patient is dead or past cure.

Let your appeal proceed from compassion and love. To jeer, scoff, and vilify are not likely ways to reform people or convert them to God. Go to poor sinners with tears in your eyes so they may see that you have earnest compassion for their case. Let them perceive it is the desire of your heart to do them good and that it is your love for their souls that forces you to speak. Say to them, "Friend, love will not permit me to see you perish. I seek nothing but your own happiness. You will have the gain and comfort if you come to Christ." If we were to go to every neighbor like this, what blessed fruit should we quickly see!

POWER OF PURE LOVE

THOMAS À KEMPIS

Hearken, my beloved brethren;
did not God choose them that are poor
as to the world to be rich in faith,
and heirs of the kingdom which
he promised to them that love him?
JAMES 2:5 ASV

Jesus has always many who love His heavenly kingdom but few who bear His cross. He has many who desire consolation but few who care for trial. He finds many to share His table but few to take part in His fasting. All desire to be happy with Him; few wish to suffer anything for Him. Many follow Him to the breaking of bread but few to the drinking of the cup of His suffering. Many honor His miracles, but few approach the shame of the cross. Many love Him as long as they encounter no hardship. Many praise and bless Him as long as they receive some comfort from Him. But if Jesus hides Himself and leaves them for a while, they fall either into complaints or into deep dejection.

Those, on the contrary, who love Him for His own sake and not for any comfort of their own, bless Him in all trial and anguish of heart as well as in the bliss of consolation. Even if He should never give them consolation, yet they would continue to praise Him and wish always to give Him thanks. What power there is in pure love for Jesus—love that is free from all self-interest and self-love!

LOVE ONE ANOTHER

ANDREW MURRAY

"My command is this:
Love each other as I have loved you."
JOHN 15:12 NIV

Christ is the Son of God's love—the bearer, revealer, and communicator of that love. His life and death were all love. Love is His life and the life He gives. He only lives to love, to live out His life of love in us, to give Himself in all who will receive Him. The Holy Spirit is the Spirit of love. He cannot impart Christ's life without imparting His love. Salvation is nothing but love conquering and entering us.

Nothing can be more natural than that Christians should love one another, even as Christ loved them. The life they received from their heavenly vine is nothing but love. This is the one thing He asks above all others: "Hereby shall all men know that you are My disciples: Love one another." As the special sort of vine is known by the fruit it bears, the nature of the heavenly vine is to be judged by the love His disciples have to one another.

Love your fellow Christians as the way to stay in the love of your Lord. Let your interaction with the Christians in your own family be holy, tender, Christlike love. Let your thoughts of the Christians around you be in the spirit of Christ's love. Let your life and conduct be the sacrifice of love—give yourself up to think of their needs, to help and to serve them. The life Christ lives in you is love. As you live out your life, let it be all love.

Scripture Index

OLD TESTAMENT

NEW TESTAMENT